Spiritual Insight

7 Sisters, 7 Continents,

7 Lessons…

Dr. Jane F. Cundy

"If you do not obtain the light of Inner Peace, mere external ease and pleasure will become a source of pain."

~ Milarepa, Buddhist Saint, 1052-1135 CE

Written By
and
Published By

Dr. Jane F. Cundy
The Business Connection Services
6024 Whisperwood CT NE
Albuquerque, NM 87109
E-mail: info@thebusinessconnection.com

© 2013, All rights reserved
All quotes are credited to their authors

ISBN: 978-0-9887414-1-6

Cover design by Judy Leahy
Original rose watercolor by Cynthia Porter
Diamond design by Dr. Jane F. Cundy

Additional Books by Dr. Cundy:

~ Lessons of the Rose…Six Steps to Personal Empowerment, Workbook, © 2002

~ Building a Business is Like Eating an Elephant…You Do it One Bite at a Time, Workbook, © 2004

~ Your Coffee Break for the Brain, A compilation of Stories, Quotes, Inspirations and Tips, © 2013   available on Amazon.com

~ 7 Sisters, 7 Continents, 7 Lessons; a Journey of Truth, © 2013

This Little Book of Truths
Is Dedicated To
Prime Source
With My Eternal Gratitude
For His Trust and Belief in me

I am in gratitude to Jane Blume for her editing skills and to Judy Leahy for her design on the cover of this book, along with their unselfish love, support and friendship. Their assistance in getting this book to you made my job so much easier and more joyful.

Introduction

"We are instructed to hold this world in balance within the land and the many universes with special prayers and ritual which continue to this day." ~ Chief Dan Evehema, Hopi Elder, 1891-1999

This book is written from a basic human level so we may better understand how "7 Sisters of the Pleiades star system, 7 Continents on planet Earth and 7 Lessons" have affected our spiritual growth, both as individuals and as civilizations.

This book is a broad brush stroke of one person's observations and spiritual insights. How is all of this connected, and what expressly is God's plan for humanity? Are we on track, or are we off on our own self-important journeys?

Originally stimulated during meditation and while pondering the news of the loss of one of the white buffalo calves, these thoughts motivated me to wonder about how many there are on the planet. The white buffalo calves are very important to the Sioux Nation and to countless other tribes, I feel a very close kinship to these marvelous creatures and I mourn when one of them has died for any reason.

As the meditation continued, the significance of these beautiful babies filtered through my mind. The question became one of how many had to collectively be on the planet to affect spiritual change and humanity's growth. Why <u>white</u> buffalo? The answer was simple: because the buffalo is a metaphor of service.

When the buffalo were killed during the early years on the Western plains, each part of the animal was used in service; whether it was meat, skins, teeth, hooves or the sinew. No part was killed for sport or for the sake of killing, and each animal was blessed and thanked for its contribution. Why white? White represents Spirit it is all inclusive. Native Americans continue these traditions of honoring all life and its sacredness.

As the Sioux refer to the buffalo, they have a particular reference of being representative of the feminine energy. Additionally, the buffalo is considered the most sacred animal for Native American Nations. According to the Sioux belief and traditions, the buffalo has virtues of chastity, productiveness and hospitality. These are the same virtues that the Sioux attribute to women. It is also true that great reverence is given to the Sioux women and great care is taken to protect women. These are traditional beliefs and are true only when honored by men. They can only be honored by all men when the society is in balance, and we are all far from that.

To keep humanity in balance, there had to be seven white buffalo calves on the planet at a time. This correlates with the Seven Sisters of the Pleiades and the seven continents. The significance of the buffalo (bison) calves is that we are all in our infancy…

This is another reason why white buffalo were chosen. It is now time in our human evolution to bring into balance both the male and female energy. Neither was originally created to be superior to another; that was man's own doing.

The Pleiades are important and hold significance to every society on this planet. There is a mystical lore and belief system to every civilization that resonates with the Pleiades. Why? What is the connection? When I conducted more research, it became clear to me that every way of life on every continent has a story that relates to the Pleiades. Thus every tradition and every continent has an aspect of the seven lessons.

I have learned over decades of spiritual training that the most important number to Prime Source is seven, and there must be seven aspects to Divine Love. This book will visit the seven aspects of Love, and how we get ourselves enmeshed in these different levels. We will better understand how we can move and grow into deeper states of unconditional love.

Our lessons continue to be how to release humankind from dual aspects throughout all of our experiences. Humanity created these aspects when we began to believe that we were not worthy of unconditional love.

So it is with each baby that is born. All babies are expressions of pure, unconditional love until they do their best to "fit in" with their families and society. It is then that each one picks up the belief in duality: the learned lessons of what we are "not." Many of us can remember this from the stories of Hans Christian Anderson; specifically the story of the Ugly Duckling (1844), who wanted to fit in and to be one of the flock.

It is our desire to be one with our own "flock" that has been the impetus for the Antarctica metaphor. We all have a tribal desire to fit in, to be one with, to be approved of, in some fashion. It is this great human need and it is the fear of not belonging that keeps us trapped in our own state of isolation and frozen tundra.

Thus the journey began. Instantly, it became clear that each of the seven stars of the Pleiades represented one of the aspects of Love… but which one? And how did all of this come together?

These beautiful buffalo are Prime Source's metaphor for balance. It means we must have seven white buffalo calves on the planet at one time, all doing well, before humanity as we know it can evolve. The metaphor is so perfect that the white buffalo calves are found in different locations, thus representing different cultures and different aspects of Divine Love.

Each ethnicity has its own beliefs and traditions for tribal acceptance. It is the human condition to require emotional love from another, however, we are not as individuals always adept at choosing our most compatible match. Many times we are so eager in our wanting that we accept the first one who shows us a modicum of acceptance or approval.

We see this all over the planet when in the news we read how one spouse has beaten up another or worse killed the partner who they once cared enough for to marry and build a life together.

How many marriages do you know that are incompatible with each other almost to the point of hate, yet people stay married to each other because of one of two reasons. The first and possibly the strongest reason is because their religion said; "til death do us part," "or that divorce within their religious structure is a sin, and they will burn in hell or at the very least, will never get to heaven. The second most popular reason for staying together is because of money. As a human culture we have kept women so subservient that many still do not have credit in their own name or are able to support themselves and possibly their children on the money that they are able to make.

While it is true that more and more women go to college and have the potential for a lucrative career, it is equally true that many more do not have either.

Humanity is seeking its way back to unconditional love, yet it has limited ideas about how to get there…or that it even exists…or that we, humanity, are not "there" already…wherever "there" is.

My research revealed that each continent was directly related to the Seven Sisters of the Pleiades. It then became obvious to me that each continent holds one of the core lessons of the seven, just as each white buffalo holds an aspect of balance. The fact that all of the white buffalo calves are present on Earth at this time is telling us that the time has to come to develop our own spiritual maturity. This choice, while deeply personal, is also collective.

Understanding how the seven sisters, seven continents and seven lessons interrelate, and how we learn from the interrelation will assist us in our spiritual growth. As many master teachers have taught, we are all in this together!

Listed next are each of the seven continents and the core lesson each one represents:

1. **North America** ~ to learn balance and the foundation of the trust in self.

2. **South America** ~ the duality of nature; the masculine and feminine energies; the split from Oneness.

3. **Europe** ~ self-worth and the value of each human; never power over, but power in unity. Power of the individual as a clear representation of Prime Source.

4. **Asia** ~ the betrayal of self. Put no other gods before me.

5. **Africa** ~ the equality of every life; building on the foundation of the self. It is the oldest civilization and is the core.

6. **Antarctica** ~ a total lack of belief in the self. Frozen in thought and beliefs; the absence of a belief in Prime Source; the beginning of duality and the bleak absence of Oneness.

7. **Australia** ~ known as Oceania; representative of spirit; the movement back into Oneness; the Ocean of Love and Mercy; the glory of the self in recognition of coming from the one and only God, Prime Source.

It is humanity that manifested five of the lessons that are being experienced and learned on each continent. It is humans who lost their way and created a return to Prime Source that is so arduous.

Prime Source/Great Spirit originally gifted us with two lessons. The first one is to trust in Prime Source and in the self. The second is to have an unconditional love for all life. The duality...the positive and the negative... came from mankind, and for millions of years we have been living out these manifestations in spades! Our greatest lessons are to incorporate the two original lessons that Prime Source gifted us with upon creation. These are our razor's edge into spiritual maturity. These are our Occam's razor.

> Occam's razor, by definition states that "it is superfluous to suppose that what can be accounted for by a few principles has been produced by many." the Summa Theologica of Thomas Aquinas (1225-1274). Quoted from Ask.com

The opposite is true for the manifestations that we have embroiled ourselves in for so long. For example, the opposite of fear is unconditional love. The opposite of anger is compassion. The opposite of worthless is worthy, etc. We, for the experience, simply got caught up in the masculine forms of energy; it came about because there was an imbalance in equality between the male and the female.

The forms of masculine energy are so familiar that to mention them is like discussing the day's news. We have for centuries been lead by the men in our lives. We have as a society and definitely as females, believed that the male species was stronger than, wiser than and even more entitled to knowing truth. This energy which is the masculine form of energy has controlled from the basis of fear and intimidation. We bear witness to this through centuries of war, rape, pillage and power struggles. It doesn't matter from which continent you came, these forms of masculine energy have ruled.

It is not about men versus women but of the polar opposites of a dualistic society. We have believed for as long as one can remember that we must live in a dualistic society. There must be bad to have good, struggle to have victory, pain and sorrow to have joy and love.

These dualistic beliefs are mankind's creation. They are the impetus for the masculine energy to maintain control. These are not the lessons from Prime Source, but the lessons learned from the warlords who came to Earth billions of years ago and attempted to control all life forms. We have emulated these behaviors and beliefs for so long that we have forgotten the original lessons of the feminine.

The feminine sides of unconditional love are compassion, humility, unconditional love, self-worth and self-love. As a national culture, we are beginning to learn the values of the core lessons depicted in Africa (building on the foundation of the self) and in North America (learning balance.)

We are beginning to build the foundation of the self and have started to care more than ever for each other. We are learning to balance our actions with caring for others. We are just beginning to balance our actions with our emotions and giving greater credence to our accomplishments. As we learn, Antarctica melts.

We are incorporating the lessons from Europe and not reigning over the people as in a monarchy, but beginning to value each human life. Even the monarchies are beginning to change and to value their people. We watched and learned as then-Princess Diana of Great Britain stepped out of the traditional role and became what continues to be known today as "the people's princess." We celebrate as Prince William, the Duke of Cambridge, and Prince Harry, his brother, carry on the work of their mother through charities and organizations benefiting humanity.

We are learning the values of each gender. We are slowly incorporating the values of the feminine both through laws and through our actions. We are beginning to stand up and take care of each other. We have recently witnessed this playing out in the actions of citizens standing up for others in recent events: at Wal-Mart, in parking lots, in auto accidents and in caring for animals, including dolphins and whales.

We are beginning to believe in ourselves as individuals and to celebrate the wisdom of children. Some have even become our teachers in the arts, the sciences and math.

We are slowly beginning to understand that there is one God, and that Prime Source is here for each person, each animal, and every other living entity. We are demonstrating our growing understanding by changing laws and policies - both nationally and state by state.

We are rebelling at the idea of going back to the Dark Ages where we pitted one against the other. We are discovering that we enjoy living in the light! We are slowly, as a world culture, beginning to value and understand the concept that neither the masculine nor the feminine is greater than the other, but are equal aspects of the Divine.

The more we embrace these principles and spiritual laws, the more Antarctica melts. Why is it melting? Because our beliefs, our attitudes and our trust in ourselves and our Creator are growing; the less frozen in these states we become, the greater our lives will expand, the healthier our bodies will be and the happier each person will become.

Antarctica's melting is not to be feared but celebrated. We will naturally move into the Oceania of life. This is not to say that change is easy, but it is something that humanity has asked for over a very long time. Prime Source always grants our requests, especially when they are beneficial for our spiritual evolution and does so in Divine Right Timing…this is it.

Table of Contents

Introduction

Lesson #1: Why the Pleiades?

Lesson #2: Frozen Dreams; Rituals and Traditions

Lesson #3: Becoming Courageous

Lesson #4: Building a Foundation

Lesson #5: Speaking Out

Lesson #6: The Value of One

Lesson #7: Divine Balance

**Chapter One
Why the Pleiades?**

Why the Pleiades? What makes them so special, as opposed to other planets and galaxies?

The Pleiades are honored and revered by almost every culture on this planet. They are mentioned in nearly every mythology and folklore. They are credited in stories that have been handed down from generation to generation by elders and shamans, parents and teachers.

According to *mythologyhttp:www.pleiad.org*, the Pleiades are among the first stars mentioned in literature. The Chinese began reporting connections to the Pleiades as far back as 2350 BC. Europeans began referencing the Pleiades in a poem by Hesiod around 1000 BC, and of course there are Homer's *Iliad* and *Odyssey*.

The fascination with star systems, and more specifically with the Pleiades, is found in the Christian Bible in the Book of Job, 9:9 and 38:31. There are, in fact, three different references to the Pleiades in the Bible; the last one is in the Book of Revelations, 1:16. It is here that they are described as, *"a vision of the coming of the Messiah-who holds in his right hand, seven stars..."*

Literature and history go on to credit the Pleiades in the Greek, Arabic, Andes, French, Incan and Mayan cultures as well as in such Native American cultures as the Cheyenne, Nez Perce and Sioux Nations.

Astronomy also has a long fascination with the Pleiades. Why, then, would we not look into this relationship as well?

Next, it became apparent that I should ask Prime Source why the Pleiades are so important to every culture, and why should we care? Why write about this?

The answers to my questions were; the Pleiades are so significant because on some of the planets within the Pleiadian star system their citizens have never lost their belief and trust in Prime Source (God.) The Pleiades, or at least some of the planets within this cluster, have maintained a clear pathway to Prime Creator.

The ancient ones (original residents) from the Pleiades hold original and core memories and experiences of their creation. The inhabitants of the other planets do not remember having the same experiences with Prime Creator or Prime Source; they are not as experienced or as evolved. They are younger in their evolution.

Every planet, including Earth, has to go through the learning processes and challenges that we humans are going through and have gone through since our beginning. The reasons citizens of Myrope never had to go through these lessons, is due to afore mentioned facts.

Learning is what happens on all planets and with all civilizations. Some take longer than others. Some simply choose to not change the way that they live, nor are they themselves willing to change.

Their elders maintain that they have long-standing traditions and experience in living this way - so why change?

Each planet has contributed to our experiences on Earth. Each one, along with the Pleiadians, contributed their "best of the best" in ideas and traditions for us to emulate and learn.

We, as humans, decided that these entities must be gods: they knew so much more than we did and after all, they told us they were!

Our rituals and traditions came from these ancient beliefs and practices. We continue these traditions today with the belief that what we are doing is what is "right." We have such a long history of experience to prove it to ourselves.

Every planet and its inhabitants started out as pure representations and expressions of the Divine. Yet, like those of us on planet Earth, the people gave their power away to those deemed smarter than they were and who they believed must be gods. After all, they said they were, remember?

Power mongers and warlords from every other planet chose to flex their presumed importance and self-inflated worth. There are always some who claim authority and power over the inhabitants of every society. These are the ones who came here as warlords with the belief that humans were never going to be smart enough to stand up for themselves and claim their God-given rights and individual worth. The distortion began.

These are the self-appointed rulers who began teaching humans to be subservient to their desires enslaving the entities on all continents so that they felt unworthy. Their ability to distort truth and gain the trust of humans was easy once Earthlings were convinced of their status as great rulers and gods.

Promoting attitudes and fostering core beliefs of lack and not of being good enough or smart enough just fed into the warlords' and power mongers' insatiable hunger for more power and control. This is how monarchies were born. This was one method of stripping Earthlings of their belief in Prime Source. It is here on this planet that we continued to hold warlords and humans in greater esteem than our Creator. This continues today in all civilizations globally.

On Earth, as well as on most other planets, the early inhabitants were known as Neanderthals. They were not only the early inhabitants of this planet, but those who criticized progress were also labeled Neanderthals. They refused to recognize and accept anything that might cause change. Their fear was so great that anything that upset the norm was too dangerous to attempt. Neanderthals are happiest with the *status quo* and never want to upset their feelings of safety or security.

Neanderthals are the ones who today still choose power over the people as opposed to working for the betterment of a society. These are also the planets that hold on to the old ways, and when they refuse to change, eventually implode.

The Pleiades are where our origins as humans began; each one of the Seven Sisters, each one of our continents that represent ritual and change, came from the Pleiadian Star Cluster, the Seven Sisters.

While it is true that many of our human brothers and sisters have inhabited other planets, like Sirius, Andromeda, Aldebaran, Arcturus and other star systems, the original point of origin was the Pleiades.

These other star systems are all very important and valued. We have all learned many lessons by having life experiences on them, however, those who are the Ancient Ones and teachers for humans today all resided originally within the Seven Sisters of the Pleiades. The original lessons were never forgotten and remain with the Ancient Ones on Myrope.

I learned in meditation and from my great mentors that as in all civilizations, whether you are from Earth or from another star system, change is not easy, and no one really wants to find a different way to do what has always been done. It is so much easier to follow in the footsteps of those before us than to carve out a new path... even if the new one might be better.

Change is so difficult for everyone that some planets are imploding and ceasing to exist because for millennia the occupants - the entities that live there - have refused to change and to grow.

Traditions and rituals are so ingrained within their individual tribes and cultures that the idea of altering or improving how something is accomplished is simply unthinkable and undoable. "This has always worked this way, so why change it?" Or, "This has never worked, so why change it now? It didn't work then, and it won't work now."

This takes place daily on our own planet Earth. Simply read the newspaper, listen to the news or follow the stories on the Internet, and you will be deluged with people from all continents and all walks of life whose feet are firmly planted in the past and in old traditions. These people are so afraid of losing what they have that anything representing change is terrifying.

My mentors also shared with me that the Ancient Ones on the planet Merope, one of the planets within the Seven Sisters star cluster, are more advanced in their ways, are readily open to change and to the evolution of ideas and events.

These beloved entities are advanced in their thinking and in their behaviors. They are not like some of the other planetary beings within the Pleiades and other star systems. These entities are on a Divine Mission. They are creating a pure pathway from Prime Source to living entities on many different planets. These entities are considered the Way Showers.

They are known as Ancient Ones. These Great Beings possess a real clarity and a purity of intent, to which the rest of us aspire. These Ancient Ones have not spent millennia questioning the intentions or desires of Prime Creator. They never chose to make themselves into gods or superior to the One who created them! These Great Beings never strayed from the original two lessons.

It was also shared with me that because these Ancient Ones have never had to go through the lessons, trials and challenges that we on Earth are going through; they have been chosen by Prime Source to come to Earth and to assist humans with our lessons and challenges.

These are the teachers that humanity has chosen to learn from and to emulate, and it is their Divine Mission to assist us and to treat us as their younger brothers and sisters.

I must also share with you that they are not here to do our work for us, but to teach, share and to provide ways of doing things that are far more supportive than we have found for ourselves in previous and current lifetimes. For example, teaching us ways to build better aircraft such as the stealth bomber or advanced radar systems are perfect examples. We have discovered treatments in health care that if not for our sisters and brothers from the star systems would not be available. These Ancient Ones and others who care and love us continue to assist in all areas of our lives bringing us closer and closer to our original mission which is being one with Prime Source, God, Great Spirit, Allah- or whatever name is most comfortable for you.

Their only purpose is to teach humans multiple ways to serve, to live a life of unconditional love for all living beings and to be of service to all humankind.

Prime Source provided us with only two commandments. Mankind, in order to have more power and control over the masses, created what became distortions from truth. Power and control began as early as the existence of time and has grown across planets into what it is today.

The first of two commandments is to trust in the self and to have complete trust in Prime Source. All of humanity continues to work on these commandments. This is one of the lessons that the Ancient Ones are here to assist us in leaning.

The second is to provide unconditional love and care for all living entities, be they human, animal, marine life, birds, or those who crawl upon the Earth. This also includes the living plants and vegetation, as all living things belong to our Creator; we simply have been gifted with their use and custodianship. We were commanded to "do no harm." These lessons, while simple in their meaning, have proven for millennia to be difficult to maintain. This commandment is also the commandment for healers. Prime Source gave this commandment to all humans, not just professional healers.

For as long as time has been recorded, humans do their best to make things harder than they need to be. You have heard the saying, "The message is simple, yet the task is not easy."

One of the most basic traits that humans from all continents seem to have in common is the ability to alter free will into power and control. For whatever reason, people seem to think that one person is more important than another. One needs to have dominion over their fellow humans… and animals!

Perhaps, the words of Black Elk, an Oglala Sioux shaman, say it best: *"Behold this day, for it is yours to make. Now you shall stand upon the center of the earth to see..."* This is a message to us all. For this day is ours to make, and the center of the Earth, Black Elk tells us, is everywhere. All we need to do is to see the world in a sacred manner and the holy tree will live again. The Oneness was never meant to be divided.

Somewhere throughout life's experiences, it has become a pattern with people to think that what they have to have must be greater than another's; there is more of an advantage, and you have greater prestige, position and authority if you have more than your neighbor.

Lame Deer, a 20th century shaman among the Sioux, had this vision of America's future: *"Listen,"* he said, *"I saw this in my mind not long ago: in my vision the electric light will stop sometime. It is used too much for TV and going to the moon. The day is coming when nature will stop the electricity. Police without flashlights, beer getting hot in the refrigerators, planes dropping from the sky, even the President can't call up somebody on the phone. A young man will come, or men, who'll know how to shut off all electricity. It will be painful, like giving birth. Raping in the dark; winos breaking into the liquor stores, a lot of destruction. People are being too smart, too clever; the machine stops and they are helpless, because they have forgotten how to make do without the machine. There is a Light Man coming, bringing a new light. It will happen before this century is over. The man who has this power will do good things too -- stop all atomic power, stop wars, just by shutting the white electro-power off. I hope to see this, but then I'm also afraid. What will be, will be."*

What is true is that we were dreamed into existence by our Infinite Creator, and each of us was endowed with most special and unique gifts.

What also is true is that each of us, no matter our role or our position, has slept and become frozen like Antarctica, forgetting just who we are and what we are about. Let's not repeat the patterns of the past. Let's instead embrace the opportunity to move forward by re-enacting the original dream and accepting the gift that once was given... yet too soon forgotten.

These dreams are the dreams of every man, woman and child. We have become small in our thinking and in our actions when it comes to how we serve, treat and honor all of humankind. The lessons of Prime Source are so simple, and yet we have become determined to make them as convoluted and difficult as possible.

Any time you buy into, "Well we've always done it that way; it didn't work then and it's not working now." You know that humanity is stuck in the traditions of the past.

We bought into the idea that one gender is greater than the other. We believed that if we treat everyone as equals, we will have to give up some of our power and control. What exactly is it that we are controlling, and what is it exactly that we have authority over?

Power is the wind or thunder. Power is the force of the river and the light from the sun. Everything else that we speak of is an illusion and a means to control what was never ours to control. It was also never ours to give away or to sell. These are all gifts from Prime Source.

Remember what started this whole journey into lack and greed. It was billions of years ago when the warlords from other planets came to Earth and we, in our ignorance and infancy, treated them like gods. They wanted to take over. They wanted control, and they still do. Humans said, "They must be right; they have more education. They have more technology. They have more of everything. We must listen to them and do as they say." It was in our very beginning that (we) humans gave our power away.

Our distortions are many and live on each continent. When we speak of the lessons of mankind, we must also notice that they all flow and run into each other. One is not more important than the other, but each one is a variation played out in dramas conducive to each continent - conducive to where humankind is in its evolution.

Every generation has given its individuality away. Every generation is "educated" to believe that someone must be smarter and more powerful. We have lived these lies for billions of years. Every individual in every culture on every continent has succumbed to these misdeeds and lies. We simply play it out through different stories, examples and traditions.

In religions it gets played out as, "My god is greater than your god." Religions of all faiths, denominations and practices do their best to buy your allegiance. You are threatened with horror stories: if you do not live by their edicts you will either burn in Hell, not be rewarded with seven virgins - or potentially just as harmful - you will live in some half-way heaven called Purgatory throughout eternity. Why?

Because according to mankind's religions and centuries of gifting leaders of all religions with an overabundance of authority, we bought the idea that we could never be "good enough" to be one with our Creator! As the old saying goes, we "bought the farm".

Yet it is mankind who delivers these threats, and I know of no priest, rabbi or imam who has actually gone to these horrendous places and come back to tell their story. There is nothing to see or witness, for these falsehoods do not exist. Let me say this loudly right now…GOD DOES NOT JUDGE!

It is mankind who forces you to cross their palms with currency so that you may buy their stories based on power and control, and you might just buy your way into what is known as Heaven.

Humankind continually tries to make our Creator one with human qualities; and yet if that were so, creation could never have taken place, because as humans we simply are not able to manifest such magnificence.

Each culture on each continent has been gifted with at least one great teacher, one great leader who has already learned the lessons necessary to assist as we humans grow and evolve.

It is also true that each master teacher walked the Earth at exactly the right time for the lessons that were needed during their incarnation. While each of these great masters had the capacity to embody both the feminine and masculine energies - true balance - their choice was to participate in a manner that was congruent with the times, and to teach the lessons that they were here to teach. It became more believable for the humans if there was a counterpart to their embodiment. Mankind needed the duality, therefore so must these great and learned teachers. Religions taught us this.

For Jesus, or Yeshua, it was his mother: Mother Mary, the embodiment of the female aspect of God or Prime Source. His best friend and companion, Mary Magdalene, walked the Earth with Him and shared His teachings with others. They never married for there was no need for such tradition. Each had their own mission and while the missions were compatible, the lessons remained separate in their presentation. It is true that they walked the Earth together teaching and sharing, but each as friends, not as a marriage partner.

Kwan Yin was for Buddha, as Mary Magdalene was for Yeshua, a great friend and teacher of the feminine. Kwan Yin continues to hold the energy of the great mother just as Yeshua's mother, Mary, continues to embody for Christians.

For Muhammad it was Khadijah. Muhammad, as did the other masters, taught that men and women were equal in the sight of God. Muhammad was also the prophet of a "one-god" belief system. Before that, many different cultures believed in over 350 gods, each one having a specific role and responsibility.

These lessons were meant to bring about the balance of God's masculine and feminine energies and to demonstrate that neither one was greater than the other, nor that either one had control over the other. God's balance is always perfect balance.

The female aspects were embodied to provide a living example of Divine Love through the feminine gifts of creativity and nurturing. They are here for the benefit of mankind's beliefs and the duality of nature. They are equal in all ways with the masculine; they simply continue to have different lessons to share.

The male expressions were a closer match to the time in which people lived. During these times females were considered property. The male was also needed to experience the balance of action and strength. They were the leaders of their communities and the caretakers of their families. They fought to provide all necessities for existing, and were the true examples of the masculinity of nature.

Not a lot has changed in our roles, except that feminine energy is claiming the right to be equal, and the masculine energy is feeling as if it is being weakened. This is far from the truth. Just as with any change, the pendulum swings to the far right and back to the far left before it settles in the middle in balance. We are in the process of discovering our balance.

When we attempt to come back to the only Power that there is, we must begin at the beginning. We have heard said that in the beginning was the WORD, and the WORD was LOVE. This being true, let us remember that the absence of this Love is what all fears are based upon. All of mankind's creations are illusions; all living things are God's creation and they are real.

Humanity on all seven continents have based their very existence on the absence of Divine Love and embraced fear to its very core. We have lived this way for billions of years and called it living successfully. Without unconditional love and a respect for all life, fear has become so much of a habit that we call it normal. We have become Antarctica.

We are so frozen in our beliefs and so enmeshed in the importance of technology and manmade machines that we have made them our gods. Greed has made money a god; and yet look what happens when priorities are skewed. Monetary systems fail, mortgages fail, and bailouts do not get bailed out. Humans even believe that they can recreate life! It is called cloning, and it will never be truly successful as life cannot exist without Spirit…God. Mankind is not GOD!

Chapter Two
Frozen Beliefs;
Rituals
and
Traditions

We hold on to traditions and rituals as firmly as if they were our mothers and fathers. Our grandparents speak of the old days and how things were so much better, life was easier and "we always did 'it' this way; we did it right."

Much like Antarctica, traditions rule societies and the old ways are the "the way it is done." They are tried and true and should not be tampered with. This is why Antarctica became so large, humanities frozen ways and beliefs never altered. The more frozen we became, the thicker the ice and the less inhabitable Antarctica became.

Scientists warn us of the dangers of global warming, and yet because of traditions and rituals and the fact that global warming has never happened in our lifetime, politicians and others dismiss the importance of their research.

Weather patterns change, volcanoes are erupting and earthquakes are occurring more often than ever before; snow accumulations and droughts manifest in record amounts and fire fighting professionals across the United States are reporting how different this year is from any other they can remember, yet the public says; "Oh, I remember this from last year. There is no such thing as global warming." Technically they are correct. There is no global warming. Gaia, mother Earth, is evolving and she is returning to her original created form. Gaia is God made and mankind cannot alter her evolution.

Politicians dispute the research and findings of world-class scientists who have devoted their lives and careers to studying the movement of the Earth, tracking the cycles of the moon and planets and documenting how the Earth is shifting on its axis (so far a little more than 5%) causing what these world-class leaders have identified as global warming. Historians can agree and it is documented how Earth is repeating a cycle that takes place approximately every 26,500 years.

There is a huge difference this time, and that is because as Antarctica melts it is a direct correlation to humankind's belief systems and our willingness to evolve. This is not what humans know of as global warming, but it is the Earth herself changing and evolving. These are Earth changes directed by Prime Source that are designed for our spiritual advancement as well as for Gaia's.

It is time for all of us to evolve and grow spiritually. Antarctica is God's metaphor for our lack in belief and trust in self and in Prime Source. The more we grow and change, and the more we return to our belief in our Creator, the more Antarctica will melt. The metaphor will no longer be needed. Her lesson will be learned.

We see this on a daily basis on the Internet and in the news as the media reminds us of how global warming is altering the Earth. Oceans are melting and animals like the polar bears, seals, sharks and others are finding it difficult to survive. Marine life is finding their way to parts of the globe that they never inhabited before as the waters warm and the tides shift.

Just recently swimmers have encountered large jellyfish, the black nettle, with tentacles up to 30 feet, maybe more. These giants of the ocean have never lived as close to the shores as they are now showing up. The reason attributed to this change by scientists is that the temperature of the water and the air continues to warm.

World news agencies provide reports of how countless amounts, types and sizes of debris from the Japanese tsunami are washing up on the shores of Washington State, Oregon and California, bringing with them life forms that have never inhabited this continent.

Scientists share stories of how marine life and animals up and down the food chain are adversely impacted. Many cannot survive because nature and their food sources have been intensely altered. This not only impacts both marine life and wildlife, but these catastrophes have also dealt blows to the economy worldwide - well into the billions of dollars.

We watched as the greed and lack of caring for human life resulted in the greatest oil spill in America's history. After billions of dollars have been spent, and humans have done their best to clean up the environment, it is the need for tourism and businesses to get back to normal that has state governments telling us that the fishing is safe and the beaches are clean. State Governments tell us the fishing beaches are clean because of the need for tourism and businesses to get back to normal. We can see with our eyes that the beaches are clean, and goodness knows I want every person to be able to make a fair living and have the ability to care for their families, but how safe can the ocean life be to eat with millions of gallons of oil on the bottom of the ocean? The food chain cycle alone would show that bottom feeders are being eaten by the next level of predators who are also consumed by the next level on the food chain. All life have had to be affected by such a disaster.

Oil simply does not dissipate, it gets to be like sludge and thickens and settles to the bottom of the ocean where the bottom feeders become infected and the story repeats itself.

Hundreds of citizens volunteer on a weekly, sometimes even on a daily basis, to walk the beaches to pick up tons of plastic and other debris. They vow to clean up the foreign matter and trash on the shores of California, Washington and Oregon. Seals, fish and birds ingest the plastic along with other forms of debris and then die. The cycle repeats itself...but it doesn't have to.

We have become so mindless and steeped in the traditions of the past that our trash is now a floating island twice as large as the state of Texas...and growing... in the Arctic Ocean. As citizens we have become the slumlords of the planet.

Traditions and rituals keep our eyes closed, our mouths shut and our separation from Prime Source at an all-time high. Many times it is those in authority, from government officials to business people, who are so vested in their own legacy that the truth is hidden, and falsehoods are perpetrated.

♦

This metaphor that I learned many years ago is a great example of how traditions can adversely impact us.

> Many, many years ago there was a tribe that lived deep in the rainforests. No one had ever encountered these natives. Civilization as we know it never caught up with them.
>
> Like all tribes, age-old traditions and rituals were an important part of their lives. It was their traditions and rituals that formed their culture, provided laws by which to live and were icons for children. Traditions spoke of how and when to advance into manhood.
>
> As the young boys reached a certain age, they were sent out into the forest with no food, water or weapons. It was their Rite of Passage into manhood and it was this ritual that determined who was ready to be called a man.
>
> These young and virile boys wore cuts on their cheeks made by the elders, and were sent out into the forest to learn how to fend for themselves.

The blood drew the wild animals to them. They now had to learn how to fend for themselves against predators. They scrounged for food and water to survive.

This tradition, this ritual, was to last thirty days. Upon their return, each one had earned his rite of passage into manhood.

This tradition was as old as the lineage of the tribe, and no one saw a reason to change it.

One particular year the boys went out as usual, and they were attacked by a pack of wild dogs. With no training or weapons, few of the boys survived to tell of the trials and deaths of the other boys.

Years went by, and fewer and fewer boys were able to survive and return due to the attacks of the wild dogs.

Finally, the elders gathered to speak of their traditions and to decide if things should change. After all, there were fewer and fewer boys to carry on and to become men and lead their village.
The elders met, sat by the fires and spoke about what to do. After many days the elders voted, and their decision was to continue on as they always had. After all, it was tradition, and it was their way of life.
It didn't take many more years before the whole tribe was wiped out. There were no young men to defend the village, and the wild dogs had become too many.

Frozen in their beliefs and in their rituals, humankind forgets where it came from and who created life to begin with. This has happened on each of our continents and within all of our cultures. These traditions and rituals are the fears and limits created by mankind; beliefs wither and trust diminishes.

Rituals and traditions do not have to be elaborate or even steeped in our past to have control over us. We all are steeped in tribal traditions.

Most of us brush our teeth in the morning upon waking. This is perhaps followed by the ritual of our morning coffee and even reading the newspaper before going to work.
The ritual stymies us when we become ingrained with the order in which these habits are executed. For instance, upon arising, I put on my morning clothes, feed my bird, feed my two dogs and when the dogs are fed, go downstairs brush my teeth. Next, I heat the water for my tea and turn on the computer. You get the idea.

The other day, I altered the order in which I did things and fed the dogs first, made the tea and then fed my bird. I totally forgot to brush my teeth! Ritual!

This is a simple illustration, but if this simple morning ritual can throw off one's day, what will happen with the large changes?

I know a woman who becomes totally thrown off her game if she doesn't rise at the same time and perform her daily chores in the traditional way, allowing the rest of her day to go smoothly. When life throws her a curve ball and the ritual changes, the rest of her day is so frustrating that it upsets her for the whole day. By the end of the day, she is exhausted!

We see this every day in our work. Managers micro-manage the performance of the employees. The work must be accomplished in specific ways and in a specific order - or it is "wrong".

Humans love to be in control, and many times have feelings of being "less than" if they have to relinquish that control to someone with greater authority. Parents force their children to perform tasks in a particular order and within a certain time frame. Lessons must be learned in a certain way or the child is regarded as inadequate, perhaps even labeled as "stupid" or "lazy". As a society we are so frozen in our beliefs and traditions that making room for the new is daunting to say the least.

We follow rituals in all areas of our lives. Our school system is so entrenched in the traditional method of learning that nationally, our children are falling behind. My own state of New Mexico currently ranks among the bottom five in education. As of this writing it is number forty-nine.

Scholastic leaders and politicians have fought for decades to maintain the same ways of teaching. Yet, teachers and entrepreneurs have been introducing advanced learning tools and processes – and they are getting astonishing results. These new methods are enhancing the learning abilities and increasing the comprehension of our children; kids are becoming smarter. Through it all, those who are stuck in tradition are stonewalling educators and political leaders because they are too afraid to make the real changes. They are more afraid of losing their position of authority and status than doing what is right for the children and the nation.

In parts of our country, parents of young children who are financially able are so concerned about the "right" day-care facilities and the best schools for their children, that babies who are less than two or three years old are signed up for the most prestigious and upscale schools possible. All of this is simply fear based. We live in the "what if it doesn't work" syndrome. Well, what if it does work, and we need not live in such fear?

Of course we all want our children to have the best education, so why not spend more effort on every school's curricula, and teach in ways that our children actually can learn - instead of adhering to the old traditional ways that have long ago been proven to be ineffective?

We don't require adults who can parrot back dates and figures; we demand leaders and free thinkers. We call for scientists and mathematicians who can think outside of the ritualistic norm and create unprecedented miracles. It is fear! Society says, "why change what doesn't work. We have always done 'it' this way." More fear!

It is more important for unions to keep teachers employed, even if they are not good teachers. Do away with tenure and stop rewarding time as opposed to talent. Begin by putting our priorities in order. We are also learning that educators who have a passion for a particular subject make better teachers because they teach from their own state of love. Children learn better, and they retain more when the teacher is excited about what they are teaching. Why not allow teachers who are passionate about math teach math, and those who love English teach English or Spanish or science or music. Imagine how creative our children will be when we return art and music to the mandatory curriculum as opposed to cutting these due to budget cuts. Our creative ability is the greatest gift we received from Prime Source. We do not require a society stripped of its creative powers. We must enhance creativity in our children so that we may continue to be the inventors and way-makers of the future.

Businesses and corporations are acting in the same manner. Millions and billions are spent rewarding top CEOs, who sent the organization into ruin, with the so-called "golden parachutes". If the person knew that he or she would do a great job and do it for the good of the people, there would be no need to worry about a golden parachute. These rewards are fear based, and greed is always based in fear. You don't have to tell people that you are doing well; do well, and they will automatically recognize you.

It wasn't until the Civil Rights movement from 1958 to 1968, and the Civil Rights Act of 1964, that African-Americans were provided equal rights, including the right to vote. At long last, traditions and rituals were overturned to allow individual rights for African-Americans who had worked, died and been tortured as they began the process of fighting for equality.

We still, as a unified country, do not fully embrace the rights of minorities, no matter what the laws say. Equality is given lip service and for the most part, humanity swallows it like it is candy!

For over 200 years we have continued to fight for the rights of all citizens no matter their beliefs, their sexual orientation or their ethnic background…and we call this the land of the free. It is only really free if you are white, male and wealthy!

It was four years after women received the right to vote that Native Americans *(1924 Indian Citizenship Act)* were granted status as citizens and obtained the right to vote.

It wasn't until 1963 that the US Supreme Court in *Gideon v. Wainwright* certified that all persons have the right to a court-appointed lawyer, if they cannot afford one. *(The Sixth Amendment to the U.S. Constitution provides the right to have an attorney.)*

It is just now, in 2013, that the Violence Against Women Act (VAWA) has finally been passed, with rights granted to all minority women who are victims of violence. Before this act was passed, the rights of minorities - Latina, Afro-American, Asian, and Native American women - were excluded.

The statistics continue to report that one in three women have been abused, either physically, sexually or emotionally. These statistics only increase when minorities are included. For so long and in so many countries it is considered the norm to punish a woman if she is not submissive to her male partner or parent. It is not much different for children all across the globe.

Women and children are still considered property in much of the world and unfortunately this also the case in the minds of men...even in America. This is especially true of women in lower income families and neighborhoods. I think that the statistics alter in these neighborhoods because women of means are more reluctant to report the abuse for fear of loss of either their families or financial support.

Native American women are three times more likely to be a victim of abuse than a woman of Anglo descent. The same is true for Native American children. Many of these crimes go unreported and unpunished due to a lack of trust in authorities, fear of reprisal or a belief that nothing will be done about the abuse or to the abuser.

Women still do not have the equal rights granted by the Equal Rights Amendment *(originally introduced in 1923)* - which was passed by Congress in 1972 - because 38 states, as is required by the Constitution, have not ratified it. Traditions, control, power. We cannot, as of 2013, even get 38 out of the 50 states to ratify the ERA, and we call this freedom!

In fact, as of 2013, we continue to fight in Congress for the rights of equal pay for women. The opposition is all based in fear and reflects our frozen beliefs and values. Antarctica at its best!

Traditions and rituals run deep throughout humanity. You can visit any culture on any of the seven continents to see just how the dysfunctional clinging to the old and maintaining our frozen values and beliefs adversely affect humanity across the planet.

Traditions and cultural values are also of great importance the Spanish or Latino communities. For instance, one's *familia,* or family is a major source of identity, individuality, and protection. It is critical to the Spanish/Latino family to feel included and to belong; in fact it is a major source of one's identity. These feelings are not only limited to the immediate family, but close friends can also be included as familia. These traditions are so ingrained within the culture that the idea of oneness, of equal value, is diminished by separating roles and responsibilities. Traditions, no matter how comfortable, keep us frozen in states of separation from the Divine. We place more importance on the human aspect and less attention on Prime Source.

These traditional forms of separation and of hierarchical importance are found in clans and tribes globally and are germane to the lessons of South America as well as Asia.
We must advance our beliefs before we can change behaviors. This only takes place when we can change the belief of one person being worthless into beliefs of everyone being worthwhile and as important to humanity as they already are to God.

It is true that members of the clan are morally responsible for the safety and assistance of the entire clan, be it financial, health related, or other issues as they arise. The father, or the eldest male if the father is not there, is primarily responsible for the protection of the family. He is also the chief decision maker for the extended family.

Mothers or the eldest female child, raises the children and is revered and protected. The eldest female has full authority of the home and this usually includes an extended family as well.

The extended family is as important as the original family of origin and depending on the environment can be quite large.

Family is always the most important consideration in any decisions.

These traditions continue throughout not only the Spanish or Latino communities, but throughout Asia, Africa and most Eastern cultures.

It is in the West that we have strayed away from such long held traditions. We are beginning to understand that each person has their unique identity and individual value. We just do not want this to swing the pendulum so far the opposite way that family loses all importance.

We can surf the Internet and scroll through story after story of human rights violations. We can read how traditions and rituals breed conflict, inflict pain and violent death... how the human expression is so entrenched in worn-out ways, in time-honored traditions and human servitude, that our memories and our values of what is true, what is kind and what love is, no longer exist.

We can look at the different continents and see how each one has played out its own stories of ritual and traditions. In Africa, for instance, the tribes continue to regard one tribe as more valuable than another; we witnessed that in Rwanda, and it continues today in Somalia and Sudan as well as Algeria - and on and on... an ongoing fight for more control and power.

Remember the core lesson from Africa is to value the self, the individual.

Al Qaeda believes that they are fighting Allah's war, and they do it from one stronghold to another. I cannot even imagine a God who would require one of Prime Source's children to believe that they are more important, more valuable or more "right" than another. If that were the case, why create the lesser, when you have the ability to create the best?

Africans fight out their version of ritual based on their beliefs and customs that go back to the beginning of recorded history. These frozen attitudes and beliefs have kept humankind looking outside themselves for answers for centuries. These are prime examples of humanity's frozen states of beliefs and rituals. Civilizations, with their time-honored traditions, have forgotten who their Creator is.

We must get to the place where we treat people as equals. One of the best pieces of advice that I received as a young adult was to always assume that the other person is <u>at least</u> as smart as I am.

For instance, over the course of history the core message of each culture has been about people who have given their individual power and their individual voice away. We have given it freely to anyone whom we believed to be more powerful, more important or smarter.

We saw this in World War II, when Hitler, who was a man of very low self-esteem, thought that the only way to achieve his self-proclaimed power and control was to annihilate anyone who was different. He attempted to create a pure class of people. It didn't take long before Hitler declared himself "Fueher." By 1933 he had already declared the Nazi Party the only political party to be acknowledged in Germany. One thing that you can say about Adolf Hitler... he was very committed to his cause.

"The fact that Hitler was able to destroy German democracy in only six months serves as a warning today of what can happen if the public is apathetic," Chancellor Angela Merkel said.

"Human rights do not assert themselves on their own; freedom does not emerge on its own; and democracy does not succeed on its own," Merkel said. "No, a dynamic society ... needs people who have regard and respect for one another, who take responsibility for themselves and others, where people take courageous and open decisions and who are prepared to accept criticism and opposition." (quotes from the article on different tyrants via the internet.)

Machiavelli once observed that one does not maintain power with the same following used to gain it. Niccolò Machiavelli strongly advocated evil, corruption, and the demoralization of the people. He taught that these elements were critical to controlling the population politically, and that ethics only got in the way.

We continue most recently with the new rule of the young testosterone driven and egomaniac leader of North Korea, Kim Jong Un. Kim Jong Un is the son of the late Kim Jong II, and grandson of the founding leader of North Korea, Kim II Sung. It seems, he has no preparation for the betterment of his countrymen, and his actions are predicated solely by his need to show his supremacy to the world. It also seems that he acts more from spontaneity and short temperedness than cool thinking and planning. Dictators and warlords all have one thing in common; no regard for human life or individual sanctity.

The Hopi Indians have long predicted what is now taking place and what is to come on our planet. The words of the elders ring as true today as they did over a thousand years ago.

The great Hopi Chief Dan Evehema tells of the future through the Hopi prophesies, and a part of what he says is here for your edification:

"...The basic premise is that humans cannot simply make their own laws and enforce them with weapons without regard to natural order. The very means of enforcement violates that order, causing precisely the suicidal situation now faced today." (Taken from Chief Dan Evehema's "Message to Mankind and the Nine signs." jahtruth.net/chiefdan.htm)

The opposite of fear is unconditional love. The opposite of anger is compassion. The opposite of worthless is worthy, and so on. We, for the experience, simply got ourselves, all of humanity, caught up in the masculine forms of energy – which resulted from the imbalance of nature and inequality among human beings.

We have played this scenario out on every continent and within every culture. In Africa we have witnessed the brutal murder and annihilation of entire tribes. As humans we tend to sit by and watch as greed takes over; certain parts of humanity decide who gets to live and thrive and who must go.

It is the same thing that has been repeated in Europe with Hitler and the annihilation of the Jews. Power was taken, and control was given.

For the last two hundred-plus years, we in America have been trying to prove that one ethnic culture, one gender or one lifestyle is better than the other. If this were true, why would our Creator waste valuable attention by creating so many variations?

Some of us continue to believe that God intended for man to be in a loving relationship only with a woman; that to live differently is an abomination of God's Law! Once again: if that were so, why then would there be those who are born with different a set of beliefs and interests and choose to live differently? Love is Love, no matter with whom you choose to celebrate it.

God created the choices and the differences. If man was to live with the same mate forever, there would be no need for different choices or lessons. Do you not think that God can create or eliminate what God chooses? If God was subject to humankind's laws, none of us would exist!

For over 151 years, with the Homestead Act of 1862 (and even before,) white men have been conquering different territories across our great land and claiming that they owned it; settling it by driving out the "savages" who cared for and loved this land far longer than any white person ever had.

The day will come when humanity will seek the wisdom of these wise ones with their ability to live with the land and with all life in harmony, and they will become the teachers for the survival of all humankind.

When the Hopi prophesies come full circle, and mankind's priorities shift, humans will once again begin to believe in the power of Nature. We will listen to those who for centuries have celebrated Great Spirit, honored all life and have given thanks for the gifts bestowed upon us by our Creator.

These wise ones will teach all of mankind how to grow crops, harvest only what is required for sustenance and care for Mother Earth and her inhabitants. They will teach us the value of herbs for healing and how to learn from our elders instead of pushing them aside.

For years white men killed the buffalo *(or North American bison)* to starve the Indians and simply for trophy and to satisfy greed. Today this continues as we form hunting groups and call it sport - all for the prize to hang on the wall. This year in

Yellowstone Park more than 350 additional buffalo were slaughtered than last year.

Ranchers are finally discovering that buffalo, along with the prairie dogs, are the great recyclers of the land. By their natural habits the soil is turned, grasses grow faster, and the richness of the land is preserved.

Without the buffalo turning the soil and the prairie dogs creating tunnels allowing for the seeding of the grasses, we would have lost the Great Plains a long time ago to mankind's greed and need to have control being more important. This is one small example of how Prime Source's Law works and how mankind's power over others causes scarcity and undue suffering.

After millions of centuries humankind continues to believe that they are more important, and God's animals have little or no value. Some people continue to believe that animals have no soul or intelligence. They believe that the animal's only value is to provide food, to be used for work and sporting pleasure.

Some are so barbaric as to believe that it is acceptable to brutalize roosters in fights to the death. This is one more example of the ignorance of humans, who are continuing to control life. Humankind continues to eliminate what and many times who get in the way of excessive profit and greed.

We are finding more and more life forms threatened with extinction because of traffickers' greed and their insatiable need for money and trophies.

In his competition for power and control, mankind has created all of the issues that we have today, not just with farming or grazing rights, but the sustenance of life as we know it.

Today mankind destroys the rain forests in his need to take. Plants and trees are being eradicated faster than we can count. Animals are poached and slaughtered so that the overly wealthy can have exotic food to eat, trophies for their walls, and the lumber companies can make their millions. Meanwhile, life forms become extinct, and the balance of nature goes unheeded. Some call the results of this global warming. Others call it progress. God calls it self-inflicted wounds and celebrates as Gaia returns to her original state, while mankind learns some valuable lessons in remembering who he is. These are a part of the core lessons learned in South America.

Civilizations fight for possession of particular turf, claiming that it was theirs to begin with. Tribes are fighting for something that was created by Prime Source and gifted to humans to care for and to treat all life as sacred.

Neighbors fight to make sure that someone's fence is exactly on the property line; no one wants to give up six inches! It continues to amaze me as individuals from all across this great planet fight for what they believe to be theirs. Isn't it interesting that none of planet Earth belongs to humans; it all belongs to Prime Source, the One who created life in the beginning?

I have been witness recently with thousands of others as we watch via webcam the birth and rearing of three eaglets thanks to the Yukon Electrical Company, Environment Yukon and the City of Whitehorse, (yecleagles.com). Nature is so perfect in her education. As hatchlings, their parents are dutiful in their responsibilities always providing food and nourishment. There is always one parent diligent in their protection and caring never leaving their young alone for extended periods of time. As they grow the parents responsibility dwindles according to the eaglet's ability to consume on their own while still being furnished with nourishment. Around the age of ten weeks or so, parents are less visible and the fledglings must practice strengthening their wings for the great flight. Just like people, the parent's greatest gift is the push. All is seamless and in rhythm with life. There is no need for stress, no need for one eaglet to be more powerful or have more than his sibling. It is all in perfect balance. Life is meant to be effortless and flowing.

Tradition, ritual, habits and the lessons from all seven continents keep humankind out of balance. Wars are fought over what is believed to be someone's religious rights. People are winning a non-essential battle and losing the war between the Light and the Dark and the illusion continues.

Chapter Three

Becoming Courageous

"Courage is seeing people as unique expressions of Prime Creator while allowing them their chosen pathway to experience life."

The feminine aspects of unconditional love are compassion, humility, unconditional love, self-worth and self-love. As a world culture we are beginning to learn the values of the core lessons depicted in Africa and North America. We are beginning to build the foundation of the self and have started to care more than ever for each other. We are learning to balance our actions with caring for others. We are just beginning to balance our actions with our emotions, therefore, providing greater credence to what we do. We are at the forefront of courage.

We are incorporating the lessons learned over centuries in Europe and Asia by not lording power over the masses as a monarchy does, but beginning to value each human life. Where did royalty come from originally? It came from the ego of the warlords. The only way humans would actually submit to warlords was if they thought that the warlords were gods, like they did with Yahweh and Jehovah.

Humans said they must be gods because "they" said they were. They took the commanding role that humans readily gave them. These warlords and civilizations wanted to control Earth and plant a flag. Humans said they must be right for they know what we do not. "They show us ways to do things that we have never even dreamed of. We will surrender our will to them as they are so much greater"; thus was the initial experience of humans relinquishing their individual self-worth to another. It is Africa's lesson, and we look to Africa to learn about the loss of human value.

These are also the lessons of North America as we attempt to recreate balance, both individually and collectively. We are learning the values of each gender. We are slowly incorporating the values of the feminine both through laws and through our actions. We are beginning to stand up and take care of each other. We have recently witnessed this in the actions of citizens protecting others in recent events: at Wal-Mart, in parking lots, in auto accidents, and in caring for animals such as dolphins and whales.

We are witnessing our children coming into this life with talents that took earlier generations years to master. Many come with math skills that mystify their teachers. Others sit at a piano or dance with the grace and wisdom of masters who came before them. Some are scientists and computer experts before they are old enough to go to high school, drive a car, or vote!

The big difference in today's young geniuses is that they also place their attention on caring for others and using their talents for the benefit of all of humanity. This is witnessed almost daily as we watch and listen to the stories via the media. We can visit You Tube® any day of the week and watch home videos of children who at very young ages, excel in music, for example. You can view one little oriental boy, who at the age of five, is performing piano concerts worldwide. His mission, as I recall, is to bring joy and opportunity to children worldwide. He wants other children to know that they have opportunities just as he does though theirs may be expressed differently.

At the age of fourteen, another young man had already built a nuclear reactor. His long range intentions are to create clean, inexpensive energy for the world. After watching the interview on NBC's Rock Plaza with Brian Williams, we learned that he has already, at fifteen, skipped college and is inventing nuclear technology so safe and so viable that our government is interested in purchasing it. His professor, according to the interview, feels that this young man is probably one of the, if not the most intelligent, persons that he has ever met. When interviewed, this young man remarked that he has so many ideas that they may not all be able to be manifested in his lifetime, but he is doing what he can, one at a time.

We are receiving the benefit of genius from these young people in all walks of life. These children, in many instances, are far more advanced than their teachers and parents. In addition to their individual and unique talents, they each have a desire to enrich humanity. Some choose to do this with how children are educated such as more "hands on" and personal experiences rather than simply reading out dated books that may or may not be accurate, depending on how many times the information has been rewritten and whose vantage point is accepted.

Others are choosing by their example, to enrich children's lives through the numerous avenues of the arts, like the three year old whose paintings are already compared to Monet´. Still others come to us with amazing gifts in math, like the brother of the fifteen year old who excels in nuclear physics. These brothers are both being educated in schools reserved for only the brightest of the brightest.

It is so interesting to learn that these children do not necessarily come from parents who also excel in these ways, but from ordinary everyday citizens like you and me. Because these children are so advanced, we must be careful to listen and learn without being so intimidated by them that we "dummy" them down to fit in. These children do not need drugs; they need understanding and adults who are not intimidated by their vast intellectual capacity.

Many times parents and educators are so intimidated or just plain overwhelmed by these children that drugs are the only way they know how to control them. Many of these children are mislabeled with ADD, attention deficit disorder or ADHD, attention deficit and hyperactive disorder, simply because they have come in to this life with so much knowledge and wisdom that they are way ahead of their parents and teachers. There is so much information within their minds that they, at their young age, have no worldly way to disseminate or manage it. The only way the adult generation currently understands how to deal with these brilliant ones is to make them fit into the molds of the past. Drug them!

We must remember to remember that God is still in charge and is providing us with these gifts and tools to better our lives and improve the planet, not destroy it.

Globally we are slowly beginning to understand that there is one God, and our Creator is here for each person, animal and living entity. We are displaying this understanding by changing our laws and policies - both nationally and state by state. We are rebelling against the idea of returning to the Dark Ages, where we pitted one against the other, and discovering that we enjoy living in the light!

We are slowly, as world cultures, beginning to value and understand that neither the masculine nor the feminine is greater than the other, but are two aspects of the Whole. A core lessons of South America.

We are attempting simultaneously to teach and to learn this in the Middle East, for instance. People are beginning to take back their autonomy slowly as they discover that each tribe has its own history, its own stories and its own pathway to the Supreme. We are reminded daily of the sacrifices individuals are making to gain their understanding of liberty.

Children are leading us into the new millennium through their visions and their creative genius. Young women like Malala Yousafzai, the 15 year-old young girl from Pakistan who was shot in the head for attending school, are standing up for the right to have an education. The feminine energy is speaking while the age-old masculine energy, who has ruled for ages, roars in fear at the thought of losing dominance over others.

We have watched Syria for over two years now as humanity, in its quest for equality, freedom and the resurgence of the feminine, fights the dark side of the masculine control. The only reason one person fights so hard for dominion is his fear. You have to be terrified to fight that hard. The best way to stop this and to change it is to send unconditional love to that person or persons. War begets war. Love begets love. These examples of placing one above another and making gods out of men are core lessons from Asia. They are being played out and hopefully un-learned throughout the world.

Fear, the absence of Love, has been the driving force of humanity's traditions for so many centuries that while people claim to choose independence, they have not an inkling of what that looks like or how to live it. Soul remembers, and is working hard to regain what was gifted to it so long ago.

When as a society individuals attempt to carve out autonomy, they require a role model. It is difficult to form something if you have no reference point for self-rule or what the lack of restrictions looks like.

When Americans were choosing to break away from England, the fights were messy and not at all coordinated, much like what Syria and Egypt are living through today. Farmers, politicians, laborers, housewives and children all take to the streets to carve out a new direction. Yet for that to take shape there must be some sort of unity. Millions of people all yelling and ranting for their idea of independence only prove to generate more chaos. Some form of collaboration and consistency must be generated for anarchy to subside and for what the populace can identify as liberty to take effect.

When I consider the independence of Americans I can get goose bumps. We have worked hard over centuries to create, modify, improve and establish what the world identifies with as freedom. As Americans we cherish our rights and the mere thought of giving any of them up cause's dissension among the masses.

Unfortunately, as Americans we have also grown lazy and mindless when it comes to maintaining all of our liberties. We, as individuals and citizens of this great country, cannot just sit on our laurels and not expect the greedy and the powerful to claim their rights as more important. Freedom is what we chose. Liberty is what we must continue to take personal responsibility for in order for America to remain strong and independent. We must maintain this with our vote and never discriminate against another. As Prime Source has reminded us time and time again…all life is equal and important.

Isn't it interesting that as the masculine claws and fights for its life in countries around the world! In Iran, Iraq, Syria and Libya, Egypt, or North Korea, Israel and Palestine, there are those who are declaring the rights and values of each person with equal intensity; the difficulty is that only "their" view of choice and equal rights are the correct ones.

Currently we can watch the evening news or scroll the Internet as Egypt fights to understand what democracy really is and how to implement it so that all citizens benefit from a self-governing society. We watch as the first democratically elected president was ousted because he thought that he could rule the people based on his personal allegiances, not what the populace in an evolving culture could follow. He may have tried his best, I do not know, but his actions proved to be just another tyrant when he forced on the citizens a new constitution and attempted to revert to Sharia Law, thus reducing the rights of women to a strict and extreme interpretation of Islamic behavior.

Sharia Law is interpreted differently among different communities. While some are very extreme, many are not. Sharia Law basically determines how Muslims conduct business and their personal lives.

Unfortunately, in the year long rule by Egypt's ex-president Morsi, who wanted to the country to revert to the more antiquated and extreme versions of the law, restriction does not bode well with those who have tasted even a smidgeon of equality. You cannot give freedoms to people and then try to take them back. It is as ineffective as giving a child a piece of candy; just when they are beginning to enjoy it, you take it away.

Citizens of Egypt have tasted a sampling of what a democratic system might be, yet in order to live within an independent society, one must stand up and speak up for their liberties. As millions of citizens protest and retaliate against authoritarianism, they are learning what it means to form a government by the people and for the people. This has never been easy or quick. We, as Americans lived through this during the Revolutionary War and the Civil War.

In the same nature, some Jews are extreme, as are some Christians. Traditionally, Christians no longer stone people to death and non-orthodox Jews generally do not wear their hair in the same manner as in days gone by. Females are granted rights that were not entertained decades ago. Today's women of the Jewish faith are allowed to study the Torah, own and run their own business, and share in religious education as well as become Rabbis and cantors.

When mankind places one gender above the other and diminishes the value of children and adults, he is placing mankind above Allah or Prime Source. The core lesson in Asia is to place no other god before Me (God.)

There are so many who believe that their rights are being threatened. Some believe that certain pieces of dirt belong to them. Yet all of Earth belongs to Prime Source. Mankind did not create anything! Religious clerics and historians follow books that they believe to be holy, and yet these very books have been translated, rewritten and edited by mere mortals more than 500 times. It just depends on the beliefs of the people rewriting them as to what becomes law! And those laws depend on what serves the clerics and historians of the times.

Unrest is, however, shaking up the Middle East, as there are still plenty of tribes and religious factions who will kill a young girl for looking at a boy or for riding in the car with someone other than her husband. She will still be killed in the name of saving her family's honor. And this is legal…*really?*

The masculine has no idea how to live, who will rule and what change means for centuries-old traditions. Someone has to be in charge. How can a society thrive if there is no dominant power? And of course, the dominant power must be male.

People think society cannot thrive if there is no rivalry for the top spot. Competition is masculine. It has been the mode of choice since before the days of chariots and lions killing the looser. The masculine cannot let go, it would actually be considered feminine, and no real man wants to be considered "girly." The feminine energy is not about women; it is about the release of unwarranted and unnecessary fears. What is fear? It is simply the absence of love.

We have watched for generations as people are tortured. We have given credence to the abuse of animals and just now are beginning to turn things around. Frequently, it is on the local level where neighbors rally to assist one another.

This is a beginning, and each experience becomes an example for the rest of us. With each example the light shines a little brighter. We have buried our precious gifts so deeply that we have forgotten what we received at our creation. We have been so busy fitting into our lives and becoming who we believed we were supposed to be that we have forgotten who we actually are.

We so easily let go of the only two laws that Prime Source gave us as life was created. We have lost trust in the self and clearly lost our connection as God's caretaker of this planet and of all life. Imagine Prime Source's degree of trust that has been granted to humankind for us to be the caretakers of what Prime Source created!

It was during these times that our intentions grew into becoming something that we really did not want; yet we felt that we had to do it to come into being accepted within our own family and our own tribe. Once more, our need to belong supersedes all else.

We continued this throughout lifetimes; always attempting to "fit in," to "belong" and to be who we believed others deemed us to be. Belonging to a tribe is better than being thought of as an outcast.

A genuine lack of individual self-worth and self-esteem grew out of these old patterns. These patterns, lacking values, became universal and affected everyone. Nations became bullies by allowing select individuals to feel important and to exert a real power over the collective.

It seemed that those with the lowest self-esteem and lack of self-worth became the most powerful; their voices needed to be louder and their desire to control and to manipulate became stronger.

We allowed ourselves to be bullied as we learned how to be "less than" in some way. We have had our self-esteem chipped and torn away and our shell of false protection has become even stronger. The process continues as those in control exert their power over everyone. We have played it out globally. Our lesson is universal and each of the continents continue to play it out according to their core lessons *(see the descriptions in the introduction)* and their own religious beliefs and traditions. People must learn the lessons in the ways that are most familiar to them, their own traditions, and their own culture; these offer better opportunities as effortlessly as one allows.

It is where one's pain can become distorted and the results are exacerbated into such violently physical acts as rape, murder, and addictions of any sort. It only takes a second for an individual's life to change. The scenario gets played out all too often in today's societies as the fear on our planet heightens and people are attempting to change. They just do not know how to change or what to change into.

Having courage to be different is scary and definitely dangerous. Balance is a difficult thing to attain, especially if it is something with which you have never lived. North America is discovering this. We in America gave our power away to those who we believed had more intelligence and abilities. We gave it to those who wanted to have the power in Congress, and we said, "OK, you do it. We elected you, so you will take care of us."
Yet when power and self-gratification took over in Congress, society did nothing in response for decades. We had to wait until the destruction was so great, and the effect on our fellow citizens was so horrific, that we finally found our voices and began to stand up, take notice and speak loudly. Now the

people are saying; "Wait a minute! That is not what we elected you to do."

The country had to get significantly out of balance before humanity began to rebel…and rebel we will. We must, as the new teachers and as individuals, gain our balance and discover what true freedom really is. When we discover our balance there will be no need to fear our neighbors and no need to stockpile weapons of destruction. We will learn to listen to ourselves and to each other out of respect and aligned intention. This one of the core lessons of North America. The world is watching to see what our young nation will do, and we will set the tone for the rest of the world to follow. The question is what example do we choose to set?

Complete power over another, whether it is individually, in cults or in tribes, generally includes some distortion of the balance between the masculine and feminine energies. Europe is grappling with how to provide power to the people and still maintain their beloved monarchies. While the monarchy's power in England, the Netherlands and in other countries has shifted over to elected governments, many people shrivel in fear of change and of losing what they have always believed their security to be. Societies have always had someone to tell them what to do and how to behave.

This continues on every continent. More and more people are crying out to be noticed, to be loved and to be valued in their own circle of friends and loved ones. This is played out as the imbalance of energies. Just like the imbalances in countries and on continents, we express these individually.

Children in Africa are walking tens of miles or more to find refuge and solace. Their families have been destroyed or even butchered. Little ones are left to fend for themselves. They are so hungry for the basics of food, love and an education that they are willing to die before they give up.

Thousands of Syrians have fled their homeland in an effort to stay alive and to discover ways to eke out a better life for themselves and their children.

♦

How did we end up distorting the foundation of self? Some of us become very controlling and feel that it is important to dictate what we believe to be right or wrong. Others become like the lonely sheep and follow whatever anyone else says so as not to make waves. Some are very outspoken and believe that their opinions are more important than others.

We all choose what the safest way is for us to get along in a world where many times we feel we have no choice. We choose the ways in which we will be heard and valued. We all have a basic instinct to be loved and heard. People are reaching for some sense of value and importance. Excessive self-importance manifests when people make worldly goods more important than Prime Source. We are living this malady out across the globe as we continue to make technology the god.

Humankind is very enthralled with the rapid pace of the computer. The lightening speed of technology and how we can so easily encroach upon another's liberties is driving humans into a robotic society. Financial gains made at the click of a mouse have become the lord of the business world. More, more, more! When do we have enough? We are pumping out more millionaires and billionaires in 2013 than have ever existed. We are so proud of our technological prowess that we have forgotten to communicate. We say to our friends and family, don't call me...text. Don't meet with me, we can all speak via computer and save time!

Let's not forget that people require emotional relationships. We must be able to feel, listen, share and love. Computers are not capable of this, and so with much focus on technology, we are killing our society. Use the tools as they are here for a reason, but remember the Creator and please put all into perspective.

This again is acted out individually or within a particular culture or as a nation. Another prime example for these lessons comes from having placed greater importance on classes of people and on gender than on Prime Source. Judgment of self and others: this is a core problem.

It is our lack of love and our lack of understanding that cause us to manifest illnesses within our bodies. Scientists have discovered that the brain has its own complete immune system, just like the rest of the body does. They are discovering that illness may be caused by our thoughts.

Doctors and scientists wonder now if our negative thinking, our anger and our emotions could be at the root of all of our diseases. What if they are right? What if we never have to have cancer? What if cancer were caused by anger, a lack of self-worth or destructive thinking? What if all diseases begin in the mind and with our thoughts, beliefs and choices? Perhaps we bring on our own destruction or our own joy. What would happen if this were true?

When we lose our self-worth, anything is possible. We must learn and feel love from someone in our life to combat the intention and emotions that can result in some form of self-destruction or harm to others.

◆

I had a roommate a number of years ago who had a sister, who we will call Crystal, was so ill that she was literally wasting away. The young woman who was only in her early twenties had given her power completely over to the doctors, whom she believed to be the higher authorities.

Crystal never assumed any responsibility for her own wellness. When the doctor gave her the diagnosis of diabetes, it was expected that the doctor would cure it. In her mind it wasn't about changing a diet, or watching sugar levels or getting some exercise. It was simply the doctor's responsibility to fix it without her assuming any of the responsibility. Eventually, Crystal literally wasted away. Her muscles began consuming her body for nourishment and eventually, she died.

This is a blatant example of someone giving her individual power and responsibility over to what she believed to be a greater authority. It wasn't the doctor's fault; he did all that he could. She just never listened to him. Her family supported her, and she refused to take any self-responsibility.

These actions are always rooted in feelings of abandonment - whether it is abandonment by families of origin, spiritual abandonment or abandonment by others (such as friends or lovers) that become the cause of our actions. The more gratification we receive from our behaviors, the longer we will continue the patterns no matter what they are.

It is our feelings of abandonment that root themselves so deeply into our psyches and our actions. It is abandonment that causes these dysfunctions to repeat themselves generation after generation. Our parents felt these same emotions and therefore they knowingly or unwittingly passed them on to us as the best way they knew how to express love.

The way that our parents and grandparents and generations before them experienced love was the way that we were taught. Sometimes, if we were fortunate, there was someone within the family circle who was centered enough to introduce ways for us to feel empowered and loved. They provided ways to show us that we are important to each other and thus a new cycle of love was introduced. Another spark was lit and the kaleidoscope of color could become just a little brighter. It was a way to chip away at that hardened clay shell of disbelief.

In everyone's life there is always someone who has been placed there to be a model for love. It may be subtle or it may be blatant, but there is always some way that Prime Creator teaches us what it means to have Divine Love. Some of us get it and others miss it. That is the experience. Just as there is always a spiritual master to open the door to unconditional love and show us the way home, there is always someone in our lives to teach us about love. Everyone deserves to have the light left on for them to come home.

We learn how to become the person our tribal society expects us to be. We do not want to rock the boat or incite reasons for us to not be accepted. This is our voyage into giving our power away to whomever will take it. Will it be our parents, our teachers, our religious leaders, our law enforcers or perhaps our friends or lovers?

Do we maneuver our new-found self and practice our abilities to be accepted by forcing ourselves on others? Do we become a rebel and fight the establishment? Do we become a shrinking violet and shut down so that no one will notice us and therefore we won't be hurt? Or, do we simply do our best just to get along?

With all of these obstacles, it takes courage and a powerful reason to become a functioning individual. Courage is standing up in the face of adversity and taking that first step. It doesn't matter if that is the right step or the wrong step; it just matters that you take the step. The only way that the step is not right for you is if it does not put you on the path that you deem important for you right now. There is no "right" or "wrong"; there is only choice - and you can always make a different choice.

I believe that we have given our individual self-worth away for so long that taking it back is an anomaly. We have no idea, first of all, that it is gone, and second, that there is a way to get it back! We genuinely believe that there are those who are more important or smarter than we are. Thus the birth of low-self-esteem!

I believe that low self-esteem is the core of all diseases and addictions. I also believe that low self-esteem is, for some of us, a real addiction. If we didn't have to have those who are more important or valuable than others, there would be no need for low self-esteem. We would all acknowledge our self-worth.

Many of us believe in our own low self-esteem for our entire lives. Others who have been shot down either verbally, emotionally or physically, choose to get back up. Low self-esteem is a behavior, not a chemical imbalance, and behaviors can change.

This takes us right back to the very beginning of humanity. Remember the warlords who we believed to be gods because they knew something that we didn't? Well, that was the birth of low self-esteem and a lack of self-worth. We have continued these patterns for so many millennia that they now feel perfectly normal. Having self-worth and self-esteem has become the exception. This was the reason for the metaphor of Antarctica! Low self-esteem keeps us frozen in the false beliefs of lack and distrust.

Remember the Pleiadians who never gave their power away, the ones who never forgot who Prime Source is and always maintained their individual value and worth? These are the real teachers from whom we must learn. These Ancient Ones are returning to teach us, to share with us and to assist us in reclaiming what has always been ours to claim. It is here, when we reclaim the self and our God-given gifts, that we enter Australia - Oceania! We aren't there yet, but we are on our way.

◆

We must stop listening to the power mongers who tricked us into believing that they needed to be the gods, the kings, queens and leaders of society. They tricked us into believing that we were fortunate to be servants to them. While this began billions of years ago, it continues today in global power struggles and among the few who believe they are to be lords over all…warlords, power grabbers.

We were not the ones deeming ourselves to be lords over all or claiming the power to send each of us to Heaven or Hell. Hell is a place that only exists in the mind. Hell was created by religions as a power to be held over the masses, and to enable the priests and those of political stature to become wealthy. Hell was created out of fear. We gave it away; no one can take what we do not willingly give.

Power mongers are the ones who are the robbers of man's wealth for their own consumption, and who today are causing the demise of the global markets. They are the ones who sabotaged the housing industry worldwide, and are the impetus behind our own Congress's inability to make decisions. They hold the country hostage to their whims while they thrive!

We have given our power away for so long that the power grabbers, the Illuminati, believe their power to be the only law. They believe that we, the rest of society, are too ignorant to handle truths and make decisions that will positively affect our lives. It would be too scary to have the majority empowered and threaten the security and position of the few. We must, according to them, promise allegiance. These are the machinations of the original warlords.

Low self-esteem, feeling bad about yourself, and a lack of self-worth, the belief that you are not worth greatness, goodness or love, are the real impetus behind these kinds of decisions. Unfortunately these individuals have for so long believed in their own power and their in-destructiveness that they have no idea what truth is. It is time to take our individual self-worth back. It is time to reclaim our gifts bestowed upon us by our Creator.

Let Antarctica melt; it will take courage to let it happen, but we can do it as long as we remember who is in charge…Prime Source!

For us to claim our self-esteem and our self-worth we are going to have to remember who we are. We must re-claim our spirituality. Self-esteem does not come from the physical form. It originates within our spirit, our soul.

The Ancient Ones from the planet Myrope are accompanying us on this voyage. They walk beside us and offer a helping hand when we stumble. They will, upon request, offer to show us easier ways to take our next step as opposed to the arduous ways in which each of us has traveled thus far. A great part of the beauty in these lessons is that there is no judgment as to what we have done or not done. There is no ridiculing the methods previously used, and certainly no one is telling you *"I told you so."* It is all about one great question that is asked of each of us time and again. "WHAT DID YOU LEARN?"

Chapter Four

**Building
Foundations**

I believe that Prime Source has said, "ENOUGH!" The time has come to learn our lessons and to get along, to value one another, and to place our priorities in order. It appears that Prime Source's desire to allow us the experience of frozen beliefs, low self-esteem and low self-worth and beating each other up (instead of learning these lessons) only lasts so long…a few billion years or so according to human time. Now it is time to get to work and learn the lessons we all came to learn. Now our lessons of balance, not superiority and competition, come into play. This is the real reason for America and for all of North America. America is in her infancy, as are all humans. We are the new teachers, but we are only a step ahead. We must learn our own lessons of honoring and trusting the self as well as honoring and trusting Prime Source plus the balance in all things.

"When we learn to say a deep, passionate YES to the things that really matter, then peace begins to settle onto our lives like golden sunlight sifting to a forest floor." – Thomas Kinkade

The more we embrace these principles and spiritual laws, the more Antarctica melts. Why? It is happening because our beliefs, our attitudes, and our self-trust and trust in our Creator are growing. The less frozen in these states we become, the greater our lives will expand, the healthier our bodies will be and the happier each person will be. We will naturally move into the Oceania of life.

As the masculine begins to shine the lights of balance and truth on itself, and as the machinations of the past begin to fall away, we will slowly move into greater states of unconditional love.

As I mentioned at the beginning, Merope's inhabitants, respectfully known as the Ancient Ones, never strayed from their belief in Prime Source as their Creator, as their giver of all life and of all of life's blessings. They have never known lack because Prime Source never created lack; only mankind did from the perspectives of low self-esteem and low self-worth. You cannot have what you believe is beyond your worth. If you believe yourself to be worthy, nothing is impossible unto you.

This opportunity is unprecedented, and with this opportunity once again comes the great gift from Prime Source. God is requesting that our fellow brothers and sisters from Merope assist us by providing insights, training and assistance in the most obvious ways.

The Ancient Ones are here to show us that we have always been worthy, that there is nothing to earn and that as children of the One God, we have these attributes as our inheritance from a benevolent parent. We are like teenagers: we want the freedom of being an adult and making our own decisions, yet we do not have the experience or the tools to make this a reality. We are floundering in our own ignorance and disbelief while at the same time gaining the experience and trust required to actually embrace true sovereignty.

All entities from every planet, including Earth, can follow their own directions and their own edicts as to what is right and what is just for them; this has always been true, but now we will know it, claim it and live it.

To allow all entities to live their own lives and to follow their own beliefs takes a tremendous amount of courage. It also takes a tremendous amount of respect, patience and unconditional love.

We watch this fight on our own shores daily. Our own congressional body of lawmakers many times cannot get out of its own way. There is such a fight between the masculine and feminine forms of energy that I wonder if even they know what they want. I do not believe that they do.

We have never before had so many women in Congress. The methods and thinking used by women is very different, and I can promise that it is unsettling for those who have been a part of the old regime. It is also unnerving for those congressional delegates from parts of our country where the ways of the past are holding on as if in a death hold. You cannot have it both ways, and if you are not solid in your own beliefs, if change is really difficult for you, then the old will win no matter what it has to do to maintain control.

We saw this in the Civil War when factions of our society held on to slavery like it was holding on to its very security while others who were more forward thinking and choosing a greater level of balance chose to fight to end slavery. That same energy is holding on to the past today. The past is familiar, it is safe and it is comfortable. New ways of doing or being are like making vegetable soup; all of the ingredients might be there, but it isn't soup yet! These are the lessons of a new nation, our nation. We must discover and implement true balance, and as we observe daily, it is a messy business.

As a parent, each of us wants the best for our children. Our desire is for them to grow into self-sufficient, responsible citizens who follow the laws of the land and yet stay true to themselves while doing so. We want them to find their passion for their life's work, to find a partner with whom they can share a life, potentially raise a family (if that is their choice) and, as the story books report, live "happily ever after."

We also, as parents, would take all of their pain, their bumps and bruises away and experience them ourselves if we could. Yet logically we know that if we do this, our children will learn nothing. Everyone must learn to walk, run and fall when necessary for their greatest personal growth. This is the cornerstone of free will.

The same is true for families, communities, states and nations. By taking free choice away from others, we cripple their ability to grow… just as we crippled our own ability to grow.

This is why countries like Syria, Iran, Israel, Palestine, Egypt, and North Korea have such problems with unrest and hunger. With warlords wielding power over them, they must come to their own state of grace and freedom. Each continent and each society must decree for themselves how they choose to live. At this time, civil unrest and revolutions are ways people on this planet know how to gain their freedom.

Americans set the bar during the Revolutionary War and again in the Civil War. As a nation, we had to discover for ourselves what we decreed freedom to be. We are still working on this. As more and more people wake up, we can provide true freedom to each individual, no matter their race, religion, sexual preference, ethnicity, etc. The greater our freedoms will become, the more Antarctica will melt and meld into wholeness. We will become closer to the "Peace that Passes All Understanding" and wars will no longer exist.

This is what the Ancient Ones from Merope have known since the beginning. We also know as parents that when our children are about to make the really big blunder, we tend to step in and provide some advice, some of our learned experience, to reduce the pain and make it less difficult to cope. Ideal parenting would be to step in only when the blunders or the old traditions fall so short of being supportive and beneficial, that interjecting assistance becomes a blessing as opposed to an intrusion.

Just as with a child - and planet Earth is a child in the sense that all of Prime Source's creations are His children - lessons must be learned individually as well as collectively. When we look at each continent we look at the different lessons that accompany them. This is not to say that none of the rest of us have these same lessons embedded in our histories; we all do. The difference is that each continent expresses its lesson differently through its cultures. They can express the lessons in their own unique ways, but each person becomes the icon for their individual expression of the lesson as well.

When we look at the analogy of parent and child, it is like having more than one child. While all children must learn the same life lessons, how they experience the learning is individualized. Again, we have free will.

When these life lessons are experienced, I have found that both as a society and as individuals we tend to be more submissive to the ones we believe hold the greatest power or authority. This process has played itself out over centuries through traditions and rituals.

It takes a lot of boldness to buck the *status quo* and to do something different. Bravery is essential if we are to change from the old into the new. We are finding this in every corner of our society.

In 2008, my fellow citizens stood up and began taking their power back by electing an African-American president. The world was shocked, excited and amazed that such a change could take place. It took an immeasurable amount of courage and strength for so many individuals to lift their voices so powerfully.

In fact, it was such a surprise that those who would keep us down and in the dark continue to fight and shout untruths. Once again, newness and the discovery of who we are is a messy process.

The people were so hungry for something new and so excited at the possibilities ahead, that the country thought the patterns and old habits would completely change in four years. It didn't get this way overnight, and it will not change course and correct itself overnight.

No matter that it took billions of years for us to get to this point. No matter that it took centuries of people of all colors, ethnicities and belief systems to throw away their individual rights. We had allowed the few to rule the many and had given our voices and rights away willingly. No matter that the majority had believed for so long that the powerful would take care of everyone; we were in shock. The people had spoken with their votes and they wanted change immediately.
Most of society thought that "They" would always have our best interests at heart, and yet the few became frightened because

the many began to speak up and to wake up. Their voices, their needs and desires began to be heard. The bottom began to fall out of ritual and tradition. It was such a shock to those in power that they vowed that a black man with a strange name would never succeed. But the voices of the many spoke louder than the shouting of the few.

Courage, strength and the power of the people are waking the sleepers up - and not as slowly as once believed. What stood for centuries as tradition quickly unraveled, and the bottom fell out of the entire system. Once more we have signs of Antarctica melting.

Who is paying the price? Globally, we are all paying the price. What we gave away was our voice and our choices, and we have little to no idea how to correct the course.

The more we live in fear, the more power we feed to the few who claimed supremacy originally. The more we fear, the more we say to the few, "You were right. We do not know how to care for ourselves, and we are not smart enough to right this ship." Fear is our nemesis.

The responsibility for righting these atrocities belongs to all who have given their sovereignty and their free will to the leaders who would take it. Once more the lesson comes home to roost. No one can take what you are not willing to give. This time the price was high and obvious. This time people were beginning to ask questions, seek answers and demand accountability from the few in control.

Four years ago, no one in authority believed that an African-American could sway the voices of the people, but the thirst was great, and the need was overwhelming. It was also time for "we the people" to quench our thirst and to reclaim our individual sovereignty - but at what price?

The few scurried from the ranks of control in the banking systems, the auto industries and the housing market so fast that it was like rats fleeing a sinking ship. Oh, they made a racket as they left, but they were too interested in protecting their own assets to put up that much of a fuss.

This reclamation takes place in personal ways as well as on a national scale. Courage, the precursor to all types of change, moves through a family or a society like the wind; sometimes it is a tornado and other times it can be a gentle breeze.

At first, it is a small step. Perhaps it is a woman leaving a marriage that was dysfunctional and even abusive. Maybe it is a child in school speaking up about being bullied, or perhaps it is an employee speaking up about inequalities on the job.

At first there is not much of a wave; people are too used to the inequalities. Then the stories began to reach television about how many children are sexually assaulted each year.

Then we hear story after story about how families abuse their children physically, sexually and mentally; how the youth scream to be heard and valued through the use of drugs and guns. This starts to gain national attention because collectively, people do not want to hear of children being tortured and abused.

No one said anything for years about bullying in school; it was just "boys will be boys," and hazing is a time honored tradition! "Oh," they said, "kids always pick on other kids; it is just the way it is." Humans turn a blind eye to all kinds of torture until there is so much of it that it is like a cultural tsunami. Tradition: it never worked before, and it won't work now.

Animals were never considered anything but property. They were treated poorly, beaten and abused by people because people, it was believed, are more important. Animals were just stupid creatures and their worth was devalued; like women, or like people of color, they were simply property. Ignorance would tell you: mankind has dominion over the land and the animals. Humans do not own anyone, nor do they own animals. Humans are God's stewards. The truth is that God has entrusted us with caring for the Earth and all of His creation. She loves us so much that She trusted us with Her greatest gifts.

♦

Years ago I read a book titled A Kinship with All Life, authored by J. Allen Boone with Paul Herman Leonard. This book was a life changer for me and can be for those who have any kind of belief that animals are not wise. The stories provide great examples of just how animals are teaching us. They offer gifts untold as well as many treasures unclaimed.

No one cared about the dog-fighting rings, the cock fighting, the betting groups and horse races that are won by drugging the horses. The more valuable the horse, the more illegal drugs are used - all due to greed, power and self-importance.

Finally, a sports superstar who grew up fighting dogs for profit made the headlines, and society was appalled! It took a major sports figure to bring to light what should have been common sense. These old traditions needed to be addressed and banned long ago. He paid the price and went to prison.
Recently he has turned his life around even to the degree that he is supporting animal humane societies and the welfare of dogs. He is a perfect example of you don't know what you don't know.

These principles of being kind to animals and to children are taught. They are not something that we come in at birth knowing automatically.

Another example of imbalance is our judicial system. Unfortunately our judicial system is created on the basis of male white supremacy. I don't mean like the Klu Klux Klan or the white supremacists of today, I mean that the white male has dominated our society and our judicial system since the constitution was written, and that it is very difficult, if not impossible, for anyone of color, women or a minority culture to actually reap just rewards.

I don't think that we, as white Americans, really ever think about this. It is just the way that system is written...and it works for us, but consider for a moment being of a minority, any minority, and how would our justice system be balanced for you? The lesson for North America and America specifically is to come into balance in all ways. We are not even in kindergarten with learning this lesson!

There is nothing on this planet that is not an education in some manner. Whether it is plants, animals or people, we all learn from each other. This is simply one additional great gift from Prime Source.

Here are perfect examples of humans beginning to wake up to the two commandments that were originally asked of us. Unfortunately, it takes some tragedy or horrific incident to wake up humanity.

Suffering from low self-esteem is the foundation of *dis-ease*; it is, I believe, the cornerstone of all illnesses. Since all *dis-ease* is created initially in the mind, it only stands to reason that when one person feels badly about him or herself, it will be the impetus for the manifestation of a variety of *dis-eases*.

Dis-ease: meaning that there is an unbalanced relationship between all parts of the body and the mind. If the body is out of balance with itself it is in some degree of *dis-ease.*

When a child is in school and the schoolmates tease and pick on her, those perpetrating the acts might mean it as fun or playing, but the person who is being attacked is in pain. This is an opportunity for *dis-ease* to take hold.

In some it might become diabetes or some other childhood *dis-ease*; perhaps it even becomes a form of a cancer. In others it may result in depression. In still others it may cause them to rise up and become the very thing that they fear; they become the bullies as a means to defend them against being terrorized.

Bullying plays out in the form of hazing: one example is the young male college student who was hazed by other students on the school bus. This young man suffered such horrific abuse that he died of heart issues.

Bullying can cause such low self-esteem that it can be a leading cause of suicide - like the university student who was taunted regarding his choice of a sexual partner. The information was sent out via social media and the student, an intelligent and talented musician, was so humiliated that he took his own life.

Dis-eases come in all forms of addiction as well. Low-self-esteem is not always recognized as the cause of addictions, yet I believe it should be included in the mix of causes.

Everyone on this planet is addicted to something. For some it is drugs, for others their drug of choice is alcohol or sex. Still others have a more acceptable addiction…chocolate. Many others are addicted to sports…the list goes on.

All of us look for something outside of ourselves to provide that "high" that we require making ourselves feel better. Low self-esteem plays itself out as a lack of self-love. A lack of self-love becomes the impetus resulting in our need to believe that almost anyone else is greater than we are.

It takes courage to step up and look yourself in the eye, to tell yourself that you are great just the way you are.

If we as humans were so balanced in our belief in ourselves and others, we would have no need to go to war. We would have no need to place others in such authority as to have control over us.

We find gratuitous control in all areas of our lives: education, religion and government are clear examples. I am not supporting anarchy or inviting you to cause social chaos, however, I am inviting you to discover for yourself how to believe in what is right for you. I am inviting you to act in a manner that is supportive of kindness, compassion and a love for all of life. After all, isn't this one of the only requests that Prime Creator has made of us?

Organized religions have a need to control their members. They have to threaten you with sin, Hell, Purgatory, denying you seven virgins, and the list continues. It is even propagated and perpetuated throughout most of the world's organized religions that only men have the ability to become the master of their (religious) spiritual beliefs and leader of the people. When did God make that choice?

Don't you ever wonder why people have a need to go through an emissary to reach the One who created them? Individuals have to appoint a person whom they believe is more influential than they are and has more clout than they do - and yet he or she was born in the same way as everyone else.

The emissary goes to school and bullies other students just like we did; he or she is good at sports or not and is either a good student or not. Then, after going to college to study the books that were rewritten by mankind well over 500 times, he becomes this holy person in charge of your spiritual life...*seriously*?

Do you in fact believe that this person knows more about God than you do? Does this person have such a direct line to the

Creator of All That Is that you cannot contact your Creator in the same manner?

Do you actually believe that confessing your acts to another human is giving you anything but absolution from another human? God never asked you to do anything but Love your Creator, to love one another and trust in God and in yourself…that's it.

Most of the time, we are so busy asking God for something and talking to God about what we perceive to be wrong with the world or with our neighbors that we forget to listen.

If you believe that God can hear your requests, why would you be willing to believe that Prime Source can't speak to you?

Why don't we spend some of our attention listening to God's answers about the course of action that would take us in the best direction?

Look at the causes of low self-esteem again. Do you not wonder why people of various religions come away with a life-long guilt and feelings of being "less than" in every way because they were born sinners? How was the minister, priest, rabbi or imam born?

A lack of self-worth is gifted to each person who attends a church, mosque, synagogue or temple. All those who attend

Christian schools as children are told day after day how they will never be good enough because they were born of sin. Somehow, as humans, we can never quite "get there."

If Prime Source created sin, we would have to also believe that our Creator created each of us to be less than in some way. If Prime Source created sin, it would negate free will. There would have to be a right and wrong way to do things as well as good or bad. Who is to say what is right or good? Who knows what is wrong or bad? If this were true, judgment would be appropriate. Yet, the law within all great books says, "judge not." I believe that mankind created sin for his self-righteousness, self-glory, power and control over others.

It takes courage to be different and to stand up for oneself. It takes a tremendous amount of courage to not be a member of the tribal society, but to follow your own heart. It takes a tremendous amount of courage and will to stand up to authority and claim your self-worth.

This does not mean breaking laws that were created in order to have an orderly society. It does mean when those in power do not follow the dictates of the majority, they need to be replaced with those who have the daring and the will of the people as their directive.

It means that caring for one another and being kind to one another is all a part of God's Divine Plan. It means that the

Golden Rule is probably one of the only real laws and rules that we need. If we focused on that one Rule, we would not need all of the "do not" laws that just create more havoc.

As a global society we are just beginning to stand up and take back our power. This is when it really gets messy. We are witnessing this all over the globe.

We see it in Egypt as citizens attempt to create – for the first time - both a society that honors its people and a democracy.

This revolution is being repeated in Libya, Syria and all across the Middle East. People want what they have never had, yet they know not what that is.

We see this in Iran and Iraq, where tribes fight to prove their worth and women fight to be more than property.

We see the opposite in Afghanistan, where some fight based on what they believe to be *jihad*, or a holy war. Yet this holy war is all about power over others. It is about my god being superior to your god; my way is right and you will never get to Heaven because you are wrong.

This false sense of superiority has ruled our planet since time began. We know that all wars have been religious wars. Does it really take the courage of a fifteen year-old girl to change the educational rights of a nation?

The United States must be careful not to impose its idea of freedom on others, as their ideas may not be the same as ours. Once again it is, "my way is the right way and you must do as I do and do as I say."

While it is true that the United States believes in freedom and individual rights, as a nation we clearly have a long way to go to provide this for each individual. Just watch as the fights over Roe v. Wade (the right to have an abortion) continue over forty years later. Pay attention to the fight for the right to love and marry whomever you want; freedom is a journey, and we are not there yet.

We will see this revolution arise in our own land as soon as people gain more courage to stand up to the leaders in Washington. People will, as they take back their self-worth and self-esteem, begin to raise their voices of choice and change even more loudly.

Those who are so polarized in their beliefs will learn to come to the middle and value the rights and wishes of all people. When this takes place, the pendulum will shift once again and we will swing to one side and then to the other before coming back to the center.

Just like change of any magnitude, there will be times of stress, lack and limit. People will fight amongst themselves, and voices will turn to anger. Anger will turn to fighting and fighting will not make winners of anyone.

Yes, Antarctica is melting!

Chapter Five

Speaking Out

We are now learning how to begin to sound our voice of individuality. We watch this through the eyes of our children. They are so distraught over the ways of the past that they are acting out in ways that our generation, as their elders, would never have been allowed to do or would have even considered doing.

The basic problem with all of this is that the elders who are listening are few and far between. I notice this in schools - whether it is locally or in other states.

Children who are being bullied are speaking out in hopes of gaining the attention of their teachers and parents as well as their local government leaders. Youngsters in the lower grades come to their parents and teachers with stories of children who make fun of them in innocuous ways that before would have gone unnoticed or unmentioned.

For instance, little girls who dismiss their schoolmates for speaking up or making statements that they do not agree with are ridiculed and made fun of.

I know of a nine year-old who is so sensitive that when her schoolmates say things in a snide voice such as, *"Why are you always saying Mary does this, or Mary does that"* - which before would have been considered "nothing" - is now considered a form of bullying…and rightly so. Children pick on others in verbally abusive ways, and we must teach all of our children respect for themselves and respect for others. This does not come as easily as one would choose, however.

For generations many of our parents and their parents before them have hazed, bullied and even ridiculed children by telling them that they are not worth it, they will never amount to anything or that they are just born on the wrong side of the tracks, in the wrong "tribe" - or simply put - are stupid!

We see this happening on all continents and in all ethnic groups. We see this because a child is born as a gay or lesbian and doesn't have the same criteria for love that perhaps you have.

We see it when individuals choose to change their identity because they are trapped in a body of the wrong gender, and to live life fully, they choose gender re-identification. No one chooses to live in a prison.

We see it in cultures that have been downtrodden for centuries and have been told by the "great white society" that they are "less than" and stupid. They are told that they are of no value because God would never make someone "like them."

We are taught by certain ethnic or religious groups that they are the "chosen ones." This is their way to make other societies or religious groups out to be "less than". This form of power mongering has been around for centuries, and the need to be "the chosen ones," was the impetus for all religious wars.

Does God really make people who are "less than"? If that were true, why would Our Creator make anything that could be minimized? This Great Entity is fully capable of creating universes, galaxies and all life forms? Why waste talent and abilities? That would be like asking Monet´ or Picasso to paint by numbers!

We were taught the same ideologies when we were children. These inferior, negative values are not what one is born with; they have to be carefully taught.

These distorted beliefs come from our past generations and have repeated themselves until now. These distortions have been played out in the form of abuses that are so horrific that to mention them here would only serve to perpetuate them.

In my parents' generation and even before that, children were taught to be quiet, not to speak for they were to be seen and not heard, and what they had to say was not worth anything anyway. Most of these children grew up in fear and were afraid to excel. These children dummied down to fit into society. Many times children dummied down to fit in with their circle of friends. If they were too smart, they would not belong. If they didn't belong, their chances of being bullied just increased.

In the years before the child labor laws, and to a great degree today, children were considered property and made to work long hours. School was not important. In some cultures this has not changed. We all know of sweat shops and factories where children are subjected to inhumane treatments.

We recently witnessed via the news media a factory in Indonesia where over one hundred workers were killed in a fire in a sweat shop environment because the doors were locked, and they could not get out.

We trust that this has changed, and yet parents continue to abuse their children. Husbands abuse wives and wives abuse husbands. While the form it takes varies, people continue to beat and kill one another; sometimes it is verbally or emotionally as opposed to physically. Why do we as humans continue to perpetuate these acts of abuse? We do this because we are retaliating against what happened to us.

If you were abused by your mother or another female as a child, it is likely that you will become an abuser yourself and retaliate against women when you grow up. If you were abused by a man, then you may choose to retaliate similarly. Abuse is always abuse, no matter to whom or by whom it is done. This abuse is not about power, as some believe. It is about retaliation for how people were treated as children. Children could not protect themselves when they were abused. Now they are in control of someone else and vengeance is theirs.

As we learn to speak out we find that there are more gangs and more teens and young people on drugs and committing violent acts. Why do you suppose that this is true? Everyone needs to be heard and listened to.

The less often children are listened to and told how they do not matter, or that they will never amount to anything, the louder their voices become. They will speak out in whatever form gets adults and figures of authority to listen. Children and adults turn to alcohol and drugs as a way to numb out and not feel the pain.

Today these children are told so often that they are not worth anything that they say to themselves, "Well, if I am not worth anything, why stick around?" And then the suicide rate among the young skyrockets. Many times one person's act is repeated by several others. The thinking is, "Well, if you do it, I will too." We see this in neighborhoods of lower-income families, and we see it where people never expected to see it: in the higher-income and more highly educated sectors. It has grown to epic proportions within Indian Country, where within some tribes the suicide rate is 19-20 times greater than anywhere else.

We see the same thing in today's workplace. Someone works his entire career to get ahead, be promoted and achieve the top rung. The hammer drops! The company is downsizing or your co-worker was promoted and it should have been you! There is nowhere to go, so what do you do?

This injustice is the impetus for workplace violence. The average person has worked on the job for fifteen or more years, only to be told that someone else is getting the position that they have worked and sacrificed for over years. People speak out in the only way that they have experienced. They retaliate against the person or persons whom they believe abused them. This often results in murder and sometimes bombings.

What is the cause behind all of these cases of abuse? FEAR!

And what is fear but an absence of love; a loss of another person caring about you, listening to you or hearing your pain. When the pain becomes that strong, violence is generally the only resort left for those who feel that they have been rejected.

These are all immature ways of speaking out. As global societies we are in the infancy stages of learning how and when to speak out and have our voices heard. We are, however, learning.

As an immature society we stumble and fall, much like a child who is learning how to walk or speak. We begin by wanting our way to be the "right" way for everyone. We believe so strongly in our position that everyone else must be wrong. These beliefs are continually played out globally. The difference is not in the "what," but in the "how."

On every continent lessons are played out based on their spiritual, cultural and traditional beliefs and customs. The word that people around the globe fear the most is CHANGE!

We are back to: *"It didn't work then, and it won't work now, but we are doing it anyway. We are doing things this way because that is <u>what</u> we know and <u>how</u> we know to do it."*

We can grow past these atrocities when we begin to believe that those who abuse are wounded. By that I mean that they are full of fear. And when someone is genuinely that full of fear, they are also narcissistic; they care more about themselves than anyone else. They tend to develop a "my-way-or-the-highway" kind of attitude. Fear, low self-esteem and negative self-worth are the fuel for these forms of devastation.

We have the ability to learn at a faster rate, if we choose to. In fact, these methods are so simple that they date back to the beginning of creation.

Prime Source said to "love one another as I have loved you." Simply put, this means to love others with no judgment as to who they are, what they believe or how they live. It means that there is no right way or wrong way; there is just choice.

As long as you are "doing no harm," the number one spiritual axiom, and issuing no judgment upon yourself or another, your voice of individuality can be loud, strong and beautiful. "Judge not" is written in every great book and taught by every faith, worldwide.

We are now taking baby steps into the Oceania of Life!

Chapter Six
The Value of One

> *"No servant is greater than his master, nor is a messenger greater than the one who sent him,"* ~John 13:16

Perhaps the quote says it all, and there is really no reason to elaborate further.

When I consider the value of one, my mind quickly flows to different acts of bravery and consideration that humans all over the world have performed: deeds we all would consider above and beyond.

Perhaps many of you would focus instantly on the military and how so many "men and women" have extended themselves, never considering the cost to their own lives.

More recently we have had example after example of the heroes within our communities who are beginning to stand up for each other in times of peril. We have to go no farther than Boston and the Patriot's Day Marathon, or Morris, Oklahoma during a devastating tornado, and as recently as this July, 2013, when once again a nation came together to support the families of nineteen fallen firefighters in the worst loss of life for firefighters since September 2011.

Others would consider the act of the beautiful fifteen year-old girl, Malala from Pakistan, who in the face of immeasurable danger got on the bus to go to school, was shot, and is now recovering. She continues to move forward to complete her education despite the same life-threatening dangers. And as a role model for the education of young girls, she is nominated for a Nobel Prize.

Just this month, July, 2013, the young Malala was invited to speak to the children at the United Nations in New York, NY. It was her sixteenth birthday. She was brilliant! Her message was loud and clear; she (and we) are stronger now because of what we have endured. She has no animosity, no hate for the Taliban who shot and almost killed her. She holds only love in her heart for the future possibilities of children worldwide. I believe that she already has the lesson learned and will become a great teacher for all of us.

We can go back in history and take deeds from all walks of life and all ethnic backgrounds and picture the sacrifice and courage of those who have deliberately left their comfort zones to be of assistance to others.

We do this because we know instinctively that every person is important and valuable to the greater whole. We know, either consciously or in our other-than-conscious awareness, that all life is sacred.

We have watched recently as emergency personnel and first responders have risked their lives to rescue dogs from lightly frozen lakes; and how just recently, first responders took a helicopter and created a wind with its rotating blades to scoot a couple of deer off a frozen lake. The deer could not stand up on their own because there was slippery ice under their hooves.

I remember as a teenager when my dog attempted to cross a frozen bay. The Coast Guard cutters had kept the channel open so that oil tankers and other large lake vessels could navigate the icy waters; but my dog, unaware of these conditions, fell into the deep and icy water. She could not climb up and out on her own as the ice was too slippery, and it was far too dangerous for anyone to walk out on the ice because the threat of falling in was just as real for a rescuer as it had been for her. Fortunately, the Coast Guard sent their cutter to rescue my dog and she was saved; another story of going above and beyond.

We have read and heard stories of how dogs and cats have alerted their human companions to house fires, thereby saving entire families from death. The list goes on, yet the common thread through all of these stories is the value of one life.

I remember learning a number of years ago that each person is so important to Prime Source, that every individual has been gifted with a unique and special attribute. It is so special and so exclusive that if people do not share or use their gifts, the world will be forever deprived of their talents.

I think about these gifts when I look at instances where entire tribes, cultures and societies have been trampled upon and their value dismissed – all for the glory of the few.

Just as we are learning from the Ancient Ones of Merope that monarchies and rulers have duped entire societies into believing that only a few had the power and the knowledge to rule over the masses, we are beginning to understand that this is only true when we give our power away to them.

We are learning that no one can take what we are not willing to give. We are not willing to give in or give up when we are strong enough within our own selves to stand up and say, "NO!"

Some individuals grow up in situations where there seems to be no way out, or where the very act of defiance can be life threatening. When this is the case it can take a whole community to rise up and make a difference.

What, then, is the price of inequality?

We see this every day in our schools. The price of inequality is found in children with inadequate educations, and teachers who are allowed to skate by and continue teaching with mediocre skills.

We watch as schools in deprived or underdeveloped neighborhoods -along with their children - are written off because the communities feel that these children are not capable of learning and excelling. Society writes them off as stupid, unworthy and unwilling. Boards of Education, in some instances, consider these children a waste of their time.

We write them off because they are living in the barrios and ghettos - the poor areas with immigrants or people of color. Perhaps they come from families whose parents are drug users or dealers, or live on welfare as the best that they can do at the time, and therefore their children are thought to never have a chance.

We have witnessed since the most recent recession how families who have lived and worked all of their lives to have a good life and through no fault of their own, are thrown from their homes and their jobs.

We watch as those who have been out of work for up to five years are unable to find employment because they are not actively working. Employers discriminate against these individuals, and sometimes even call them lazy. Many of these are people well educated and have been responsible all of their lives, only to be caught up in the greed and selfishness of the few.

We have watched those who chose to make billions on the backs of their fellow citizens: those whose golden parachutes are so great that the value of their fellow citizens pales in comparison to their desires. We stand by as those with such avarice go unpunished, while the financial institutions that helped cause this financial ruin rake in untold wealth.

We fall victim to the people in our small towns who we felt we knew and could count on: people who - once the town elected them to care for the financial welfare of the community - fiscally raped their fellow citizens without concern for their well-being. Ponzi schemes are a dime a dozen in this day and age.

I have witnessed in the marriages of people I have known over the years how in some instances the wife gives her power to the husband, just as in times of yore, by following generations where women had less importance or were considered property. The only things changed are the subtleties with which the power is given and taken.

Conversely I have watched how the husband willingly sacrifices his own individuality for harmony with his wife. In either case, one is sacrificing their own personality, individuality and authority for the sake of the other. This habit, identified as tradition, then gets passed on to the children and the behavior continues from generation to generation.

Many times this is unconscious behavior and if you asked a person, they would strongly deny their actions. Other times, their excuse is; *"I am doing it to keep peace in the family."* Is that something that one should have to do?

We harshly judge those who have religious views that are different from ours, or families who struggle because they have jobs that pay less than a living wage. How many times have you heard that "they" won't go to Heaven because "they" do not adhere to the "right" religion, they are not following God's law?

If so many different "faiths" claim themselves to be the one and only and the right one, who then will end up as the wrong one? Perhaps individuals are written off because they were adopted or come from a country where injustices are a part of the everyday life. If these people come from "that" place, then certainly they also must be one of "them."

We watched this during World War II when American citizens were placed in prison camps because they were of Japanese descent. At the time we were so afraid of the Japanese people that everyone became our enemy, even those who were Americans and born in America.

We saw it in the 1950's when movie producers and actors were accused of being communists. Many were banned from the entertainment business, and arrested on false charges simply because they held different and unpopular beliefs.

Sometimes it was simply because someone wanted them out of the entertainment field for the sake of their own greed. We see it today, anytime someone who is different from us attempts to move into our neighborhoods or work in our company or send their children to our schools.

We saw it in the 1960's with the Civil Rights marches in Montgomery, Alabama and in Canton, Mississippi, as examples.

We were appalled when Martin Luther King, Jr. was assonated. Everyone remembers Dr. King for his "I Have a Dream," speech yet it too has fallen on deaf ears as we continue to fight for the equality promised in the writing of the Declaration of Independence. We celebrate Dr. King's legacy with a national holiday, yet we haven't altered our discriminatory policies against those who are different from us…not really. We just talk a good game.

It was 1954 when the momentous Supreme Court decision of *Brown v the Board of Education* finally ended the segregation of schools. The country rose up in disbelief when Medgar Evers, Secretary for the NAACP, received national attention as a Civil Rights activist. He fought for voter- registration rights and end of segregation of public schools. He was denied admission to the University of Mississippi Law School in 1954, even after the Brown v Board of Education decision. It was Medgar Evers who, even after his death, was instrumental in the eventual desegregation of "Ole Miss," The University of Mississippi that took place in 1962. (www.history.com)

How did we reward these brave leaders and fighters for liberty and justice for all? We did what we do to all saviors and heroes… we killed them!

We are so afraid of ourselves that if anyone looks different or is a different color or practices a different religion we are right there to discriminate against them.

In 1955 a young African American boy of 14 years was accused of harassing a White woman. Days later her relatives were accused of brutally beating before killing the 14 year old Emmett Till before disposing of his body in a nearby river. These White relatives were acquitted by an all White jury. It was acts like these and so many more that galvanized activists nationwide. (history.com/emmett-till)

Today we especially see it if the one who is different is of the Muslim faith. We are so good at placing everyone into the same category or knowing that we are "better than," "greater than" or simply the chosen ones. If you are the chosen ones, where does that leave the rest of us? Once again, power over the people!

The price of inequality is too great to measure. Just notice how far away we are from the original commandment of "love one another as you would love yourself."

Here then is the lesson to be learned on every continent and by each person through their cultures, beliefs and customs.

We must now learn the lesson of each person's God-given value: never use power over the people. Utilize your influence with and for the people. You have heard the saying, "The whole is greater than the sum of its parts?" We evolve by making the whole greater.

With this belief in place there would be no poverty, no warfare and no need to victimize others. We could live in the peace that all nations aspire to.

The symbol of Antarctica would become unnecessary and life would flow like a beautiful ocean. Water is our spiritual life force, and as Antarctica melts, water is increased. Spirit is enhanced throughout the planet as she is cleansed and purified, returning to her God essence. We will return to the Oceania of Life. We will go home.

Chapter Seven

Divine Balance

"...Faith Hope and Charity and the Greatest of These is LOVE!"
~ written in all of the great books

We speak of Divine Balance, Divine Love or Divine Intervention. We go to our respective churches or places of worship on the specified day of the week and claim our devotion and love. Each faith has its own special day set aside to pray and to pay homage to the Divine.

I remember as a child all of the people crowding into the Sunday service dressed in their best attire and listening intently as the minister or preacher would tell everyone how they needed to do better, be better and give more.

Everyone vowed to do better, and then as soon as the service was over the petty differences arose and divisiveness returned. Sometimes it happened within minutes of leaving the building; other times it waited until Monday. I used to call these people Sunday Christians or Sunday believers.

We have for so long craved the spotlight of power and recognition that we have as a global culture forgotten who is really in charge.

I have been watching the news of the new Pope, Pope Francis the 1st, who was recently elected by those in power at the Vatican. I have to say that I am in awe of his grit and courage to change the patterns of tradition. Rituals that have been in place for thousands of years are being broken in a single act. Who else has had the audacity to wash the feet of twelve inmates within a juvenile facility…much less the feet of a female and of an Islamist! SALUTE! I cheered as he stepped out on the balcony, breaking with the traditions of the past by wearing his simple cross and speaking off the cuff instead of using the canned speech prepared by those "in the know." I celebrated as Pope Francis the 1st chose to live simply in an apartment as opposed to the opulence of the papal residence. He paid his very own hotel bill where he stayed before being elected Pope. "WOW!" I said, "This is a true man of God; he is putting the people first, not the institution." He definitely has provoked the traditionalists into uproar and I thank GOD for that! This is a man who emulates the one whose name he chose; Francis of Assisi, the Saint who served mankind and all life. Saint Francis, the man who cared for animals as much as he did for humankind. This is a step into Divine Balance. How far will Pope Francis the 1st go in dismantling centuries-old traditions? I do not know; I do, however, feel that he will take it as far as he can handle it himself, and as far as he believes that the faithful can change back into putting people before brick and mortar. He will take it as far as Prime Source has asked him to take it.

Divine Intervention: this is, in my opinion, a perfect example of the first steps to change.

♦

I remember as a single mother wondering how I would teach my sons to be good citizens, to treat people as they themselves would choose to be treated. I wondered how I would teach them about diversity and how all people are valuable. It occurred to me that teaching them to have a love for all life and to have a great sense of humor would be the best tools that I could share.

I taught them as small children to not take themselves too seriously. I wanted them to know that people come in all different shapes, sizes, colors and that many have abilities far greater than their perceived disabilities.

I wanted them to know that women are equal to men, that either gender can make huge errors in life, and that they are also capable of doing great things when given the opportunity. I wanted them to learn that if you fall, you can pick yourself up and start over if you have to, or at the very least, keep going. I wanted them to learn that there is no right or wrong, simply different ways to address issues and opportunities. Whichever way serves you best is the "right" way for you and if it causes problems or stymies you in some fashion, then for you it is the "wrong" way.

I didn't know if this was beneficial at the time. I wasn't aware enough then to know that I was teaching these two young boys all about Divine Balance and Divine Love. Yet, I can say some forty plus years later, that I am proud of the men my sons have become.

We claim to be God-loving people. Then we tell those who attend our religious institutions to fear God, all the while telling these same people that God is a loving, forgiving and benevolent God. What a mixed message! You cannot have it both ways.

As Christians you are told that God's only Begotten Son died for your sins, yet pastors continue to preach that each person is born in sin. How can these statements both be true?

We preach that we are all children of the Most High, yet God only had one son… truly? Who then, are the rest of us, and how can we be identified as children of God? How can we really get to what is known as Heaven if we are never quite good enough? I just wonder…

We continue to make God in man's own image because we cannot possibly conceive of One so great as to never judge, who always accepts us for whatever we do or say, and loves us no matter what atrocity we have perpetuated upon our fellow humans or animals.

This concept of an ever-loving God is beyond the understanding of humankind, and so we continue to create a God that fits our image of what a God must be. To top it off, because we have never been able to accept a female as being as important as a man, we make God a male. If God is only male, why then is there a need for the female? Is it just to manifest more males?

If we, as some cultures do, continue to kill the female babies, who then is going to be left to give birth to the precious males?

◆

At the start of this book I introduced you to the planet of Merope. We learned that these citizens have never forgotten who their Creator is and how to live life in balance.

I am aware that these Ancient Ones live in peace and harmony to degrees that we as humans can only begin to imagine. The human race is beginning to choose peace over war. We are at our infancy,
yet under the tutelage of these Great Ones the potential for peace is greater than ever. Globally we would love it if everyone had enough food, shelter, health and prosperity. We really do not want to live with the ravages of illness and poverty that this world of warring and greed has produced and tolerated over centuries.

On Merope, each life is valued as a sacred creation from Prime Source. Each life is honored for the gifts it bestows upon its society.

There is no war. There is no hunger, and the animals are cherished for their wisdom and their role in the cycle of life. There is no need to kill animals or other life forms; no entity need give their life for others to eat. Food is there for the asking.

Plants, crops and trees flourish because there is no drought. There is no drought because there is no fear. The rivers and the mountains were never re-routed to serve mankind's desires; therefore there is no need for the planet to redirect the flow back to its origin.

Minds are not dulled by the influx of radioactive particles, and fear is not perpetuated via their media in over 20,000 endless messages a day. Count them for yourself it is endless propaganda and fear.

There is no need to propagate fear because these beloved entities have never forgotten who they are. They exist in harmony because each one is an example of Divine Love: love for one another as a unique creation of Prime Source.

Their color, size, gender or job is simply that. No one is "greater than", and no one is "less than"; everyone has their own talents, and they are celebrated as individuals. There is no need for a hierarchy when there is no need for power or class. Each job is valued and specific to the individual's abilities and desire to serve.

These sound like fantasies, and yet when our global society turns the corner on judgment of self and others, when emotional jealousies are replaced with Divine Love that is understood, there will be no need for war, people will not starve and illness will be eradicated. Why? Because all *dis-eases* are created first in the mind, then manifested in the body as a way for the body to tell us how out of balance we really are. We must learn to listen to the wisdom of our bodies for wellness to occur.

When each individual is allowed to be the expression of life that they choose to be, there will be no reason for anyone to feel "greater than" or have a need for power over others.

People will live in harmony when they begin to value themselves, to stop judging themselves and honor who they are as children of a most Benevolent Being. Abundance is ours for the asking; we simply forget to ask.

Humankind was entrusted with the care and love of this planet and so far, as custodians, we have done a pretty poor job.

We can turn this around as soon as people forget the need to be right and embrace the right to get along. We are on the pathway to Divine Balance and Divine Love, and we must now ask for Divine Intervention to make this happen.

I am choosing to embrace each of us in Divine Love, and I ask continually for Divine Intervention especially in the places on our abundant planet where there is so much anger, *dis-ease* and greed.

I ask for Divine Intervention so that we all may move gently and lovingly back into the Oceania of Life.

I pray that we will quickly learn to listen to the Ancient Ones' teachings and learn to effortlessly model their behaviors and embrace their unwavering beliefs.

John Denver said it best in his song when he sang, "love is a light that shines from heart to heart." And so it is.

**May Prime Creator
Bless Each of You
and Hold You
Gently and Lovingly
in the Palm of
(His or Her) Hand!**

Epilogue

This book was an inspiration from Prime Source and a request by this Great Deity to write these lessons down in the language of everyday people. I am very grateful that the information written here is presented by me from Prime Creator. I can only trust that I have brought this information through in its most accurate and honest form.

Some of the information is new, and some of you probably have heard it at some time in your experiences and teachings. If you find this information useful to you, I am pleased. If not, feel free to pass it along to whomever you believe may benefit from it.

There is nothing grandiose about the requests that Prime Source has asked of us. No one needs to have a college education, a Ph.D. or the like. The requests made of us are always of a very simple nature.

I have learned over the course of my life that all requests, when they are of the utmost value, are always simple in their design. It seems that the more sophisticated the requests, the more convoluted they become to carry out. It also seems that only humankind can make things so onerous.

♦

For many years I have been privileged to share in people's lives who exemplify great talent. I have been witness to artists whose paintings bring the light and sound of God into manifestation. I have had the pleasure of walking in the woods with them while they scoped out the perfect place in which to bring God's bounty into artistic expression. While these artists immersed themselves in their creative juices, I was able to sit among the trees listening to the sounds of life. The birds summer chorus, the wind gently spanking the trees all the while plunging myself in my own creative zone for writing while basking in warm sunlight.

It was during these times that I first began my writing attempts. It started as poetry. Not great poetry, but the best that a novice could muster. These quiet times are favorite memories of mine. These are examples of how simple pleasures in life can bring about the most incredible experiences.

Life is straightforward, and we as humans do our best to convolute things. I used to wonder how to manifest the experiences or the things in my life that seem most important to me. I would come up with all of these formulas, incantations, and affirmations. I would be religious in their repetition following them to the letter; after awhile these methods become exhausting and, in my experience, rarely worked.

Like many others, I followed different religious paths always seeking out what I believed to be truth. I would follow these teachings until the questions arose once more as to what is true, what is real. When the longing for truth became greater than the teachings of the day, I would seek the next level of truth for me.

My stepping stones for discovery were always preempted with learning that those in charge of the particular teaching evoked limits as to how far one could reach or how one gender was continually more important, more advanced or privy to secrets that the rest of the membership could only hope to achieve. Generally these limits were described as numbers via initiations. No matter the number or the level of accomplishment set by the so called masters, and the influential are constantly male, you always had more to achieve before you were "good enough." If female, it is unachievable in this lifetime.

Finally, one day I asked Prime Source for the best way to achieve what I was attempting. Simple was the answer. Desire, Ask, Receive, and Believe. That is the sacred formula and it works every time.

We have heard from many sources and over many years, "...and a child will lead us." I also remember reading a book titled, "All I Really Need to Know I Learned in Kindergarten" by Robert Fulghum *(Random House 1986, first printing)*. These are examples of how simple our life lessons really are.

It is my great wish that the information held in this book can be of service to those who read it, and that by awakening to the truth you might actually embrace what it is that Prime Creator has asked of us.

Just imagine: if we all embraced one lesson completely we would be half way to embracing both of them, as there are really only two great lessons to learn and to embrace.
1. Love and Trust in Yourself and in Prime Source.

2. Love all Life unconditionally and DO NO HARM.

Like humans, the Earth is definitely changing, shifting and evolving - much like a woman in labor. Gaia is making her labor pains known and is speaking to us through earth changes, earthquakes, erupting volcanoes, rising waters, melting glaciers and large destructive storms. These are just a few of the ways in which Gaia is saying that it is time for her to evolve into her next phase as well.

Gaia will evolve. She will reshape herself and reclaim the original shape of her land and water. She has to, so that as a living entity she can take her next step just as Prime Creator is inviting each of us to take our next step in our own evolution.

As Gaia shifts and changes, there will be more water in areas now covered by land. As you already know, Gaia is primarily a water planet; you are aware that our bodies are over 80% water. We are made of the same ingredients as Gaia, and we are in this together. As Gaia grows and evolves, Antarctica melts allowing Spirit to take over. We will gradually revert to our original state. These floods and glacier melts are not negative occurrences; they are clear signs that we are embracing who we are as spiritual beings in a human experience. These Earth changes are the promise of the change that we as humans have asked for over the millennia.

The more we believe, and the less we fear, the more gentle the changes will be, physically, emotionally, and globally.

I am inviting you to believe in yourself, to believe in Prime Creator and to trust that all is in Divine Right Order.

Prime Creator asked that you receive this information so that our change and growth may be as gentle on each of us as we will allow it to be.

Thank you for participating.

Dr Jane

Meet Dr. Jane F. Cundy

Dr. Jane Cundy has been an international speaker, facilitator, coach, consultant, and instructor for over twenty years. She has had the privilege of teaching multi-cultural and multi-lingual audiences.

She is a Master of Neuro-Linguistics, an International Mediator, a Certified Master Negotiator and a Doctor of Divinity. Dr. Jane is also a Registered Corporate Coach and Certified Business Coach. She combines these skills in her teaching to create an atmosphere of safety and focus of direction and collaboration. Dr. Jane's clients always complete their process by obtaining mutual resolution.

In 2010 she created and presented five courses specifically designed for law enforcement professionals. All classes have been certified for Continuing Education Credits across the western United States.

In October 2002, Dr. Cundy was invited to speak at the 3rd Annual China-U.S. Conference on Women's Issues in Beijing.

Dr. Jane has previously authored three self-published books: "Lessons of the Rose...Six Steps to Personal Empowerment"; "Eating the Elephant Workbook," designed for building a small business from inception; and "Your Coffee Break for the Brain," a collection of stories, quotes, tips and inspirations offering the reader a short break in a hectic life.

www.ingramcontent.com/pod-product-compliance
Lightning Source LLC
Chambersburg PA
CBHW042304150426

43197CB00001B/7